2 5⁰⁰ AC
3
OE

D1171263

The
Old Franciscan Missions
of California

Photograph by Howard Tibbitts, San Francisco.

MISSION SAN LUIS REY, PARTLY RESTORED.

Photograph by Fred Twogood, Riverside.

MISSION SAN LUIS REY.
Showing monastery recently built behind the old Mission arches.

The
Old Franciscan Missions
of California

BY

GEORGE WHARTON JAMES

Author of "In and Around the Grand Canyon," "Heroes of
California," "Through Ramona's Country," Etc.

With Illustrations from Photographs

MILFORD HOUSE
BOSTON

Library of Congress Cataloging in Publication Data

James, George Wharton, 1858-1923.
  The old Franciscan missions of California.

  A condensation of the author's In and out of the ol⸱
missions of California.
  Reprint of the 1913 ed. published by Little, Brown,
Boston.
  1. Spanish missions of California. 2. Franciscan
in California. I. Title.
F864.J23 1973   271'.3'009794   73-4860
ISBN 0-87821-116-0

This Milford House book is an unabridged
republication of the edition of 1913.
Published in 1973 by Milford House Inc.
85 Newbury Street, Boston, Massachusetts
Library of Congress Catalogue Card Number: 73-4860
International Standard Book Number: 0-87821-116-0
Printed in the United States of America

Dedication

To those good men and women, of all creeds and of no creed, whose lives have shown forth the glories of beautiful, helpful, unselfish, sympathetic humanity:

To those whose love and life are larger than all creeds and who discern the manifestation of God in all men:

To those who are urging forward the day when profession will give place to endeavor, and, in the real life of a genuine brotherhood of man, and true recognition of the All-Fatherhood of God, all men, in spite of their diversities, shall unite in their worship and thus form the real Catholic Church:

Especially to these, and to all who appreciate nobleness in others I lovingly dedicate these pages, devoted to a recital of the life and work of godly and unselfish men.

Foreword

THE story of the Old Missions of California is perennially new. The interest in the ancient and dilapidated buildings and their history increases with each year. To-day a thousand visit them where ten saw them twenty years ago, and twenty years hence, hundreds of thousands will stand in their sacred precincts, and unconsciously absorb beautiful and unselfish lessons of life as they hear some part of their history recited. It is well that this is so. A materially inclined nation needs to save every unselfish element in its history to prevent its going to utter destruction. It is essential to our spiritual development that we learn that

" Not on the vulgar mass
    Called ' work,' must sentence pass,
  Things done, that took the eye and had the price ;
  O'er which, from level stand,
  The low world laid its hand,
  Found straightway to its mind, could value in a
    trice."

It is of incalculably greater benefit to the race that the Mission Fathers lived and had their fling of divine audacity for the good of the helpless aborigines than that any score one might name of the " successful captains of industry " lived to make their unwieldy and topheavy piles of gold. With all their faults and failures, all their ideas of theology and education, — which we, in our assumed superiority, call crude and old-fashioned, — all their rude notions of sociology, all their errors and mistakes, the work of the Franciscan Fathers was glorified by unselfish aim, high motive and constant and persistent endeavor to bring their heathen wards into a knowledge of saving grace. It was a brave and heroic endeavor. It is easy enough to find fault, to criticize, to carp, but it is not so easy to *do*. These men *did!* They had a glorious purpose which they faithfully pursued. They aimed high and achieved nobly. The following pages recite both their aims and their achievements, and neither can be understood without a thrilling of the pulses, a quickening of the heart's beats, and a stimulating of the soul's ambitions.

This volume pretends to nothing new in the way of historical research or scholarship. It is merely an honest and simple attempt to meet a real and popular demand for an unpretentious work that shall give the ordinary tourist and reader enough of the history of the Missions to make a visit to them of added interest, and to link their history with that of the other Missions founded elsewhere in the country during the same or prior epochs of Mission activity.

If it leads others to a greater reverence for these outward and visible signs of the many and beautiful graces that their lives developed in the hearts of the Franciscan Fathers — their founders and builders — and gives the information needed, its purpose will be more than fulfilled.

In most of its pages it is a mere condensation of the author's *In and Out of the Old Missions of California*, to which book the reader who desires further and more detailed information is respectfully referred.

PASADENA, CALIFORNIA, April, 1913.

Contents

CONTENTS

List of Illustrations

The Old Franciscan Missions of California

———◆———

CHAPTER I

HISTORICAL INTRODUCTION

In the popular mind there is a misapprehension that is as deep-seated as it is ill-founded. It is that the California Missions are the only Missions (except one or two in Arizona and a few in Texas) and that they are the oldest in the country. This is entirely an error. A look at a few dates and historic facts will soon correct this mistake.

Cortés had conquered Mexico; Pizarro was conqueror in Peru; Balboa had discovered the South Sea (the Pacific Ocean) and all Spain was aflame with gold-lust. Narvaez, in great pomp and ceremony, with six hundred soldiers of fortune, many of them of good families and high social station, in his five specially built vessels, sailed to gain fame, fortune and the fountain of perpetual youth in what we now call Florida.

Disaster, destruction, death — I had almost

said entire annihilation — followed him and scarce
allowed his expedition to land, ere it was swal-
lowed up, so that had it not been for the escape
of Cabeza de Vaca, his treasurer, and a few others,
there would have been nothing left to suggest
that the history of the start of the expedition was
any other than a myth. But De Vaca and his
companions were saved, only to fall, however,
into the hands of the Indians. What an unhappy
fate! Was life to end thus? Were all the hopes,
ambitions and glorious dreams of De Vaca to
terminate in a few years of bondage to degraded
savages?

Unthinkable, unbearable, unbelievable. De
Vaca was a man of power, a man of thought. He
reasoned the matter out. Somewhere on the
other side of the great island — for the world then
thought of the newly-discovered America as a
vast island — his people were to be found. He
would work his way to them and freedom. He
communicated his hope and his determination to
his companions in captivity. Henceforth, regardless of whether they were held as slaves by the
Indians, or worshiped as demigods, — makers
of great medicine, — either keeping them from
their hearts' desire, they never once ceased in
their efforts to cross the country and reach the
Spanish settlements on the other side. For eight
long years the weary march westward continued,
until, at length, the Spanish soldiers of the Viceroy of New Spain were startled at seeing men

who were almost skeletons, clad in the rudest aboriginal garb, yet speaking the purest Castilian and demanding in the tones of those used to obedience that they be taken to his noble and magnificent Viceroyship. Amazement, incredulity, surprise, gave way to congratulations and rejoicings, when it was found that these were the human drift of the expedition of which not a whisper, not an echo, had been heard for eight long years.

Then curiosity came rushing in like a flood. Had they seen anything on the journey? Were there any cities, any peoples worth conquering; especially did any of them have wealth in gold, silver and precious stones like that harvested so easily by Cortés and Pizarro?

Cabeza didn't know really, but —, and his long pause and brief story of seven cities that he had heard of, one or two days' journey to the north of his track, fired the imagination of the Viceroy and his soldiers of fortune. To be sure, though, they sent out a party of reconnaissance, under the control of a good father of the Church, Fray Marcos de Nizza, a friar of the Orders Minor, commonly known as a Franciscan, with Stephen, a negro, one of the escaped party of Cabeza de Vaca, as a guide, to spy out the land.

Fray Marcos penetrated as far as Zuni, and found there the seven cities, wonderful and strange; though he did not enter them, as the uncurbed amorous demands of Stephen had led to

his death, and Marcos feared lest a like fate befall
himself, but he returned and gave a fairly accurate account of what he saw. His story was not
untruthful, but there are those who think it was
misleading in its pauses and in what he did not
tell. Those pauses and eloquent silences were
construed by the vivid imaginations of his listen-
ers to indicate what the *Conquistadores* desired, so
a grand and glorious expedition was planned, to
go forth with great sound of trumpets, in glad
acclaim and glowing colors, led by his Superior
Excellency and Most Nobly Glorious Potentate,
Senyor Don Francisco Vasquez de Coronado, a
native of Salamanca, Spain, and now governor
of the Mexican province of New Galicia.

It was a gay throng that started on that wonderful expedition from Culiacan early in 1540.
Their hopes were high, their expectations keen.
Many of them little dreamed of what was before
them. Alarcon was sent to sail up the Sea of
Cortés (now the Gulf of California) to keep in
touch with the land expedition, and Melchior
Diaz, of that sea party, forced his way up what is
now the Colorado River to the arid sands of the
Colorado Desert in Southern California, before
death and disaster overtook him.

Coronado himself crossed Arizona to Zuni —
the pueblo of the Indians that Fray Marcos had
gazed upon from a hill, but had not dared approach — and took it by storm, receiving a wound
in the conflict which laid him up for a while

and made it necessary to send his lieutenant, the Ensign Pedro de Tobar, to further conquests to the north and west. Hence it was that Tobar, and not Coronado, discovered the pueblos of the Hopi Indians. He also sent his sergeant, Cardenas, to report on the stories told him of a mighty river also to the north, and this explains why Cardenas was the first white man to behold that eloquent abyss since known as the Grand Canyon. And because Cardenas was Tobar's subordinate officer, the high authorities of the Santa Fé Railway — who have yielded to a common-sense suggestion in the Mission architecture of their railway stations, and romantic, historic naming of their hotels — have called their Grand Canyon hotel, *El Tovar*, their hotel at Las Vegas, *Cardenas*, and the one at Williams (the junction point of the main line with the Grand Canyon branch), *Fray Marcos*.

Poor Coronado, disappointed as to the finding and gaining of great stores of wealth at Zuni, pushed on even to the eastern boundaries of Kansas, but found nothing more valuable than great herds of buffalo and many people, and returned crestfallen, broken-hearted and almost disgraced by his own sense of failure, to Mexico. And there he drops out of the story. But others followed him, and in due time this northern portion of the country was annexed to Spanish possessions and became known as New Mexico.

In the meantime the missionaries of the Church

were active beyond the conception of our modern minds in the newly conquered Mexican countries.

The various orders of the Roman Catholic Church were indefatigable in their determination to found cathedrals, churches, missions, convents and schools. Jesuits, Franciscans and Dominicans vied with each other in the fervor of their efforts, and Mexico was soon dotted over with magnificent structures of their erection. Many of the churches of Mexico are architectural gems of the first water that compare favorably with the noted cathedrals of Europe, and he who forgets this overlooks one of the most important factors in Mexican history and civilization.

The period of expansion and enlargement of their political and ecclesiastical borders continued until, in 1697, Fathers Kino and Salviaterra, of the Jesuits, with indomitable energy and unquenchable zeal, started the conversion of the Indians of the peninsula of Lower California.

In those early days, the name California was not applied, practically speaking, to the country we know as California. The explorers of Cortés had discovered what they imagined was an island, but afterwards learned was a peninsula, and this was soon known as California. In this California there were many Indians, and it was to missionize these that the God-fearing, humanity-loving, self-sacrificing Jesuits just named — not Franciscans — gave of their life, energy and love. The names of Padres Kino and Salviaterra will long live in the annals of Mission history for their devotion to the spiritual welfare of the Indians of Lower California.

The results of their labors were soon seen in that within a few years fourteen Missions were established, beginning with San Juan Londa in 1697, and the more famous Loreto in 1698.

When the Jesuits were expelled, in 1768, the Franciscans took charge of the Lower California Missions and established one other, that of San Fernando de Velicatá, besides building a stone chapel in the mining camp of San Antonio Real, situated near Ventana Bay.

The Dominicans now followed, and the Missions of El Rosario, Santo Domingo, Descanso, San Vicenti Ferrer, San Miguel Fronteriza, Santo Tomás de Aquino, San Pedro Mártir de Verona, El Mision Fronteriza de Guadalupe, and finally, Santa Catarina de los Yumas were founded. This last Mission was established in 1797, and this closed the active epoch of Mission building in the peninsula, showing twenty-three fairly flourishing establishments in all.

It is not my purpose here to speak of these Missions of Lower California, except in-so-far as their history connects them with the founding of the *Alta* California Missions. A later chapter will show the relationship of the two.

The Mission activity that led to the founding of Missions in Lower California had already long been in exercise in New Mexico. The reports of

Marcos de Nizza had fired the hearts of the zealous priests as vigorously as they had excited the cupidity of the *Conquistadores*. Four Franciscan priests, Marcos de Nizza, Antonio Victoria, Juan de Padilla and Juan de la Cruz, together with a lay brother, Luis de Escalona, accompanied Coronado on his expedition. On the third day out Fray Antonio Victoria broke his leg, hence was compelled to return, and Fray Marcos speedily left the expedition when Zuni was reached and nothing was found to satisfy the cupidity of the Spaniards. He was finally permitted to retire to Mexico, and there died, March 25, 1558.

For a time Mission activity in New Mexico remained dormant, not only on account of intense preoccupation in other fields, but because the political leaders seemed to see no purpose in attempting the further subjugation of the country to the north (now New Mexico and Arizona). But about forty years after Coronado, another explorer was filled with adventurous zeal, and he applied for a charter or royal permission to enter the country, conquer and colonize it for the honor and glory of the king and his own financial reward and honorable renown. This leader was Juan de Oñate, who, in 1597, set out for New Mexico accompanied by ten missionary padres, and in September of that year established the second church in what is now United States territory. Juan de Oñate was the real colonizer of this new country. It was in 1595 that he made a contract with the

Viceroy of New Spain to colonize it at his own expense. He was delayed, however, and could not set out until early in 1597, when he started with four hundred colonists, including two hundred soldiers, women and children, and great herds of cattle and flocks of sheep. In due time he reached what is now the village of Chamita, calling it San Gabriel de los Españoles, a few miles north of Santa Fé, and there established, in September, 1598, the first town of New Mexico, and the second of the United States (St. Augustine, in Florida, having been the first, established in 1560 by Aviles de Menendez).

The work of Oñate and the epoch it represents is graphically, sympathetically and understandingly treated, *from the Indian's standpoint*, by Marah Ellis Ryan, in her fascinating and illuminating novel, *The Flute of the Gods*, which every student of the Missions of New Mexico and Arizona (as also of California) will do well to read.

New Mexico has seen some of the most devoted missionaries of the world, one of these, Fray Geronimo de Zarate Salmeron, having left a most interesting, instructive account of " the things that have been seen and known in New Mexico, as well by sea as by land, from the year 1538 till that of 1626."

This account was written in 1626 to induce other missionaries to enter the field in which he was so earnest a laborer. For eight years he worked in New Mexico, more than 280 years ago. In 1618 he was parish priest at Jemez, mastered the Indian language and baptized 6566 Indians, not counting those of Cia and Santa Ana. " He also, single-handed and alone, pacified and converted the lofty pueblo of Acoma, then hostile to the Spanish. He built churches and monasteries, bore the fearful hardships and dangers of a missionary's life then in that wilderness, and has left us a most valuable chronicle." This was translated by Mr. Lummis and appeared in *The Land of Sunshine.*

The missionaries who accompanied Juan de Oñate in 1597 built a chapel at San Gabriel, but no fragment of it remains, though in 1680 its ruins were referred to. The second church in New Mexico was built about 1606 in Santa Fé, the new city founded the year before by Oñate. This church, however, did not last long, for it was soon outgrown, and in 1622, Fray Alonzo de Benavides, the Franciscan historian of New Mexico, laid the foundation of the parish church, which was completed in 1627. When, in 1870, it was decided to build the stone cathedral in Santa Fé, this old church was demolished, except two large chapels and the old sanctuary. It had been described in the official records shortly prior to its demolition as follows: " An adobe building 54 yards long by 9½ in width, with two small towers not provided with crosses, one containing two bells and the other empty; the church being covered with the *Crucero* (the place where a church takes the form of a cross by the side chapels), there are two large separate chapels, the one on the north side dedicated to Our Lady of the Rosary, called also 'La Conquistadorea;' and on the south side the other dedicated to St. Joseph."

Sometime shortly after 1636 the old church of San Miguel was built in Santa Fé, and its original walls still form a part of the church that stands to-day. It was partially demolished in the rebellion of 1680, but was restored in 1710.

In 1617, nearly three hundred years ago, there were eleven churches in New Mexico, the ruins of one of which, that of Pecos, can still be seen a few miles above Glorieta on the Santa Fé main line. This pueblo was once the largest in New Mexico, but it was deserted in 1840, and now its great house, supposed to have been much larger than the many-storied house of Zuni, is entirely in ruins.

It would form a fascinating chapter could I here tell of the stirring history of some of the Missions established in New Mexico. There were martyrs by the score, escapes miraculous and wonderful. Among the Hopis one whole village was completely destroyed and in the neighborhood of seven hundred of its men — all of them — slain by their fellow-Hopis of other towns, simply because of their complaisance towards the hated, foreign long-gowns (as the Franciscan priests were called). Suffice it to say that Missions were established and churches built at practically all of the Indian pueblos, and also at the Spanish settlements of San Gabriel and Santa Cruz de la Canyada, many of which exist to this day.   In Texas, also, Missions had been established, the ruins of the chief of which may be visited in one day from the city of San Antonio.

CHAPTER II

RIGHTLY to understand the history of the Missions of the California of the United States, it is imperative that the connection or relationship that exists between their history and that of the Missions of Lower California (Mexico) be clearly understood.

As I have already shown, the Jesuit padres founded fourteen Missions in Lower California, which they conducted with greater or less success until 1767, when the infamous Order of Expulsion of Carlos III of Spain drove them into exile.

It had always been the intention of Spain to colonize and missionize Alta California, even as far back as the days of Cabrillo in 1542, and when Vizcaino, sixty years later, went over the same region, the original intention was renewed. But intentions do not always fructify and bring forth, so it was not until a hundred and sixty years after Vizcaino that the work was actually begun. The reasons were diverse and equally urgent. The King of Spain and his advisers were growing more and more uneasy about the aggressions of the Russians and the English on the California or rather the Pacific Coast. Russia was pushing down from the north; England also had her establishments there, and with her insular arrogance England boldly stated that she had the right to California, or New Albion, as she called it, because of Sir Francis Drake's landing and taking possession in the name of " Good Queen Bess." Spain not only resented this, but began to realize another need. Her galleons from the Philippines found it a long, weary, tedious and disease-provoking voyage around the coast of South America to Spain, and besides, too many hostile and piratical vessels roamed over the Pacific Sea to allow Spanish captains to sleep easy o' nights. Hence it was decided that if ports of call were established on the California coast, fresh meats and vegetables and pure water could be supplied to the galleons, and in addition, with *presidios* to defend them, they might escape the plundering pirates by whom they were beset. Accordingly plans were being formulated for the colonization and missionization of California when, by authority of his own sweet will, ruling a people who fully believed in the divine right of kings to do as they pleased, King Carlos the Third issued the proclamation already referred to, totally and completely banishing the Jesuits from all parts of his dominions, under penalty of imprisonment and death.

I doubt whether many people of to-day, even

though they be of the Catholic Church, can realize what obedience to that order meant to these devoted priests. Naturally they must obey it — monstrous though it was — but the one thought that tore their hearts with anguish was: Who would care for their Indian charges?

For these ignorant and benighted savages they had left their homes and given up all that life ordinarily means and offers. Were they to be allowed to drift back into their dark heathendom?

No! In spite of his cruelty to the Jesuits, the king had provided that the Indians should not be neglected. He had appointed one in whom he had especial confidence, Don José Galvez, as his *Visitador General*, and had conferred upon him almost plenary authority. To his hands was committed the carrying out of the order of banishment, the providing of members of some other Catholic Order to care for the Indians of the Missions, and later, to undertake the work of extending the chain of Missions northward into Alta California, as far north as the Bay of Monterey, and even beyond.

To aid him in his work Galvez appealed to the Superior of the Franciscan Convent in the City of Mexico, and Padre Junipero Serra, by common consent of the officers and his fellows, was denominated as the man of all men for the important office of Padre Presidente of the Jesuit Missions that were to be placed henceforth under the care of the Franciscans.

This plan, however, was changed within a few months. It was decided to call upon the priests of the Dominican Order to take charge of the Jesuit Missions, while the Franciscans put all their strength and energy into the founding of the new Missions in Alta California.

Thus it came to pass that the Franciscans took charge of the founding of the California Missions, and that Junipero Serra became the first real pioneer of what is now so proudly denominated " The Golden State."

The orders that Galvez had received were clear and positive:

" Occupy and fortify San Diego and Monterey for God and the King of Spain." He was a devout son of the Church, full of enthusiasm, having good sense, great executive ability, considerable foresight, untiring energy, and decided contempt for all routine formalities. He began his work with a truly Western vigor. Being invested with almost absolute power, there were none above him to interpose vexatious formalities to hinder the immediate execution of his plans.

In order that the spiritual part of the work might be as carefully planned as the political, Galvez summoned Serra. What a fine combination! Desire and power hand in hand! What nights were spent by the two in planning! What arguments, what discussions, what final agreements the old adobe rooms occupied by them must have heard! But it is by just such men that

JUNIPERO SERRA.

Founder and First Padre Presidente of the Franciscan Missions of California.

From the Schumacker crayon.

MAP OF THE COAST OF CALIFORNIA, SHOWING THE
FRANCISCAN MISSION ESTABLISHMENTS.

Map originally made for Palou's Life of Padre Junipero Serra, published
in Mexico in 1787.

great enterprises are successfully begun and executed. For fervor and enthusiasm, power and sense, when combined, produce results. Plans were formulated with a completeness and rapidity that equalled the best days of the *Conquistadores*. Four expeditions were to go: two by land and two by sea. So would the risk of failure be lessened, and practical knowledge of both routes be gained. Galvez had two available vessels: the " San Carlos " and the " San Antonio."

For money the visitor-general called upon the Pious Fund, which, on the expulsion of the Jesuits, he had placed in the hands of a governmental administrator. He had also determined that the Missions of the peninsula should do their share to help in the founding of the new Missions, and Serra approved and helped in the work.

When Galvez arrived, he found Gaspar de Portolá acting as civil and military governor, and Fernando Javier Rivera y Moncada, the former governor, commanding the garrison at Loreto. Both were captains, Rivera having been long in the country. He determined to avail himself of the services of these two men, each of them to command one of the land expeditions. Consequently with great rapidity, for those days, operations were set in motion. Rivera in August or September, 1768, was sent on a commission to visit in succession all the Missions, and gather from each one all the provisions, live-stock, and implements that could be spared. He was also to pre-

vail upon all the available families he could find
to go along as colonists. In the meantime, others
sent out by Galvez gathered in church furniture,
ornaments, and vestments for the Missions, and
later Serra made a tour for the same purpose.
San José was named the patron saint of the expedition, and in December the "San Carlos" arrived at La Paz partially laden with supplies.

The vessel was in bad condition, so it had to be
unloaded, careened, cleaned, and repaired, and
then reloaded, and in this latter work both Galvez
and Serra helped, the former packing the supplies for the Mission of San Buenaventura, in
which he was particularly interested, and Serra
attending to those for San Carlos. They joked
each other as they worked, and when Galvez
completed his task ahead of Serra he had considerable fun at the Padre Presidente's expense. In
addition to the two Missions named, one other,
dedicated to San Diego, was first to be established.
By the ninth of January, 1769, the "San Carlos"
was ready. Confessions were heard, masses said,
the communion administered, and Galvez made
a rousing speech. Then Serra formally blessed
the undertaking, cordially embraced Fray Parron,
to whom the spiritual care of the vessel was in-
trusted, the sails were lowered, and off started
the first division of the party that meant so much
to the future California. In another vessel Galvez
went along until the "San Carlos" doubled the
point and started northward, when, with gladness

in his heart and songs on his lips, he returned to still further prosecute his work.

The fifteenth of February the " San Antonio," under the command of Perez, was ready and started. Now the land expeditions must be moved. Rivera had gathered his stock, etc., at Santa Maria, the most northern of the Missions, but finding scant pasturage there, he had moved eight or ten leagues farther north to a place called by the Indians Velicatá. Fray Juan Crespí was sent to join Rivera, and Fray Lasuen met him at Santa Maria in order to bestow the apostolic blessing ere the journey began, and on March 24 Lasuen stood at Velicatá and saw the little band of pilgrims start northward for the land of the gentiles, driving their herds before them. What a procession it must have been! The animals, driven by Indians under the direction of soldiers and priests, straggling along or dashing wildly forward as such creatures are wont to do! Here, as well as in the starting of the " San Carlos " and " San Antonio," is a great scene for an artist, and some day canvases worthy the subjects should be placed in the California State Capitol at Sacramento.

Governor Portolá was already on his way north, but Serra was delayed by an ulcerated foot and leg, and, besides, he had not yet gathered together all the Mission supplies he needed, so it was May 15 before this division finally left Velicatá. The day before leaving, Serra established the Mission of San Fernando at the place of their departure, and left Padre Campa in charge.

Padre Serra's diary, kept in his own handwriting during this trip from Loreto to San Diego, is now in the Edward E. Ayer Library in Chicago. Some of his expressions are most striking. In one place, speaking of Captain Rivera's going from Mission to Mission to take from them " whatever he might choose of what was in them for the founding of the new Missions," he says: " Thus he did; and altho it was with a somewhat heavy hand, it was undergone for God and the king."

The work of Galvez for Alta California was by no means yet accomplished. Another vessel, the " San José," built at his new shipyard, appeared two days before the " San Antonio " set sail, and soon afterwards Galvez went across the gulf in it to secure a load of fresh supplies. The sixteenth of June the " San José " sailed for San Diego as a relief boat to the " San Carlos " and " San Antonio," but evidently met with misfortune, for three months later it returned to the Loreto harbor with a broken mast and in general bad condition. It was unloaded and repaired at San Blas, and in the following June again started out, laden with supplies, but never reached its destination, disappearing forever without leaving a trace behind.

The " San Antonio " first arrived at San Diego. About April 11, 1769, it anchored in the bay, and

SERRA MEMORIAL CROSS, MONTEREY, CALIF.

SERRA CROSS, ON MT. RUBIDOUX, RIVERSIDE, CALIF.

Under which sunrise services are held at Easter and Christmastide.

Photograph by C.C. Pierce & Co., Los Angeles.

SERRA STATUE.

Erected by Mrs Leland Stanford, at Monterey.

STATUE TO JUNIPERO SERRA.

The gift of James D. Phelan, in Golden Gate Park, San Francisco.

awakened in the minds of the natives strange feelings of astonishment and awe. Its presence recalled to them the " stories of the old," when a similar apparition startled their ancestors. That other white-winged creature had come long generations ago, and had gone away, never to be seen again. Was this not to do likewise? Ah, no! in this vessel was contained the beginning of the end of the primitive man. The solitude of the centuries was now to be disturbed and its peace invaded; aboriginal life destroyed forever. The advent of this vessel was the death knell of the Indian tribes.

Little, however, did either the company on board the " San Antonio " or the Indians themselves conceive such thoughts as these on that memorable April day.

But where was the " San Carlos," which sailed almost a month earlier than the " San Antonio "? She was struggling with difficulties, — leaking water-casks, bad water, scurvy, cold weather. Therefore it was not until April 29 that she appeared. In vain the captain of the " San Antonio " waited for the " San Carlos " to launch a boat and to send him word as to the cause of the late arrival of the flagship; so he visited her to discover for himself the cause. He found a sorry state of affairs. All on board were ill from scurvy. Hastily erecting canvas houses on the beach, the men of his own crew went to the relief of their suffering comrades of the other vessel. Then the crew of the relieving ship took the sickness, and soon there were so few well men left that they could scarcely attend the sick and bury the dead. Those first two weeks in the new land, in the month of May, 1769, were never to be forgotten. Of about ninety sailors, soldiers, and mechanics, less than thirty survived; over sixty were buried by the wash of the waves of the Bay of Saint James.

Then came Rivera and Crespí, with Lieutenant Fages and twenty-five soldiers.

Immediately a permanent camp was sought and found at what is now known as Old San Diego, where the two old palms still remain, with the ruins of the *presidio* on the hill behind. Six weeks were busily occupied in caring for the sick and in unloading the " San Antonio." Then the fourth and last party of the explorers arrived, — Governor Portolá on June 29, and Serra on July 1. What a journey that had been for Serra! He had walked all the way, and, after two days out, a badly ulcerated leg began to trouble him. Portolá wished to send him back, but Serra would not consent. He called to one of the muleteers and asked him to make just such a salve for his wound as he would put upon the saddle galls of one of his animals. It was done, and in a single night the ointment and the Father's prayers worked the miracle of healing.

After a general thanksgiving, in which exploding gunpowder was used to give effect, a consultation was held, at which it was decided to send back the " San Antonio " to San Blas for supplies, and for new crews for herself and the " San Carlos." A land expedition under Portolá was to go to Monterey, while Serra and others remained at San Diego to found the Mission. The vessel sailed, Portolá and his band started north, and on July 16, 1769, Serra raised the cross, blessed it, said mass, preached, and formally established the Mission of San Diego de Alcalá.

It mattered not that the Indians held aloof; that only the people who came on the expedition were present to hear. From the hills beyond, doubtless, peered and peeped the curious natives. All was mysterious to them. Later, however, they became troublesome, stealing from the sick and pillaging from the " San Carlos." At last, they made a determined raid for plunder, which the Spanish soldiers resisted. A flight of arrows was the result. A boy was killed and three of the new-comers wounded. A volley of musket-balls killed three Indians, wounded several more, and cleared the settlement. After such an introduction, there is no wonder that conversions were slow. Not a neophyte gladdened the Father's heart for more than a year.

CHAPTER III

THE MISSIONS FOUNDED BY PADRE JUNIPERO SERRA

SAN DIEGO MISSION founded, Serra was impatient to have work begun elsewhere. Urging the governor to go north immediately, he rejoiced when Portolá, Crespí, Rivera, and Fages started, with a band of soldiers and natives. They set out gaily, gladly. They were sure of a speedy journey to the Bay of Monterey, discovered by Cabrillo, and seen again and charted by Vizcaino, where they were to establish the second Mission.

Strange to say, however, when they reached Monterey, in the words of Scripture, " their eyes were holden," and they did not recognize it. They found a bay which they fully described, and while we to-day clearly see that it was the bay they were looking for, they themselves thought it was another one. Believing that Vizcaino had made an error in his chart, they pushed on further north. The result of this disappointment was of vast consequence to the later development of California, for, following the coast line inland, they were bound to strike the peninsula and ultimately reach the shores of what is now San

EASTER SUNRISE SERVICE; 1913, UNDER SERRA CROSS, MT. RUBIDOUX, RIVERSIDE, CALIF.

Photograph by C.C. Pierce & Co., Los Angeles.
MEMORIAL TABLET AND GRAVES OF PADRES SERRA, CRESPI, AND LASUEN, IN MISSION SAN CARLOS BORROMEO, CARMEL VALLEY, MONTEREY.

Francisco Bay. This was exactly what was done, and on November 2, 1769, one of Portolá's men, ascending ahead of the others to the crest of a hill, caught sight of this hitherto unknown and hidden body of water. How he would have shouted had he understood! How thankful and joyous it would have made Portolá and Crespí and the others. For now was the discovery of that very harbor that Padre Serra had so fervently hoped and prayed for, the harbor that was to secure for California a Mission " for our father Saint Francis." Yet not one of them either knew or seemed to comprehend the importance of that which their eyes had seen. Instead, they were disheartened and disappointed by a new and unforeseen obstacle to their further progress. The narrow channel (later called the Golden Gate by Frémont), barred their way, and as their provisions were getting low, and they certainly were much further north than they ought to have been to find the Bay of Monterey, Portolá gave the order for the return, and sadly, despondently, they went back to San Diego.

On the march south, Portolá's mind was made up. This whole enterprise was foolish and chimerical. He had had enough of it. He was going back home, and as the " San Antonio " with its promised supplies had not yet arrived, and the camp was almost entirely out of food, he announced the abandonment of the expedition and an immediate return to Lower California.

Now came, Serra's faith to the fore, and that resolute determination and courage that so marked his life. The decision of Portolá had gone to his heart like an arrow. What! Abandon the Missions before they were fairly begun? Where was their trust in God? It was one hundred and sixty-six years since Vizcaino had been in this port, and if they left it now, when would another expedition be sent? In those years that had elapsed since Vizcaino, how many precious Indian souls had been lost because they had not received the message of salvation? He pleaded and begged Portolá to reconsider. For awhile the governor stood firm. Serra also had a strong will. From a letter written to Padre Palou, who was left behind in charge of the Lower California Missions, we see his intention: " *If we see that along with the provisions hope vanishes, I shall remain alone* with Father Juan Crespí and hold out to the last breath."

With such a resolution as this, Portolá could not cope. Yielding to Serra's persuasion, he consented to wait while a *novena* (a nine days' devotional exercise) was made to St. Joseph, the holy patron of the expedition. Fervently day by day Serra prayed. On the day of San José (St. Joseph) a high mass was celebrated, and Serra preached. On the fourth day the eager watchers saw the vessel approach. Then, strange to say, it disappeared, and as the sixth, seventh and eighth days passed and it did not reappear again, hope seemed to sink lower in the hearts of all but Serra and his devoted brother Crespí. On the ninth and last day — would it be seen? Bowing himself in eager and earnest prayer Serra pleaded that his faith be not shamed, and, to his intense delight, doubtless while he prayed, the vessel sailed into the bay.

Joy unspeakable was felt by every one. The provisions were here, the expedition need not be abandoned; the Indians would yet be converted to Holy Church and all was well. A service of thanksgiving was held, and happiness smiled on every face.

With new energy, vigor, and hope, Portolá set out again for the search of Monterey, accompanied by Serra as well as Crespí. This time the attempt was successful. They recognized the bay, and on June 3, 1770, a shelter of branches was erected on the beach, a cross made ready near an old oak, the bells were hung and blessed, and the services of founding began. Padre Serra preached with his usual fervor; he exhorted the natives to come and be saved, and put to rout all infernal foes by an abundant sprinkling of holy water. The Mission was dedicated to San Carlos Borromeo.

Thus two of the long desired Missions were established, and the passion of Serra's longings, instead of being assuaged, raged now all the fiercer. It was not long, however, before he found it to be bad policy to have the Missions for the Indian neophytes too near the *presidio*, or barracks for the soldiers. These latter could not always be controlled, and they early began a course which was utterly demoralizing to both sexes, for the women of a people cannot be debauched without exciting the men to fierce anger, or making them as bad as their women. Hence Serra removed the Missions: that of San Diego six miles up the valley to a point where the ruins now stand, while that of San Carlos he re-established in the Carmelo Valley.

The Mission next to be established should have been San Buenaventura, but events stood in the way; so, on July 14, 1771, Serra (who had been zealously laboring with the heathen near Monterey), with eight soldiers, three sailors, and a few Indians, passed down the Salinas River and established the Mission of San Antonio de Padua. The site was a beautiful one, in an oak-studded glen, near a fair-sized stream. The passionate enthusiasm of Serra can be understood from the fact that after the bells were hung from a tree, he loudly tolled them, crying the while like one possessed: " Come, gentiles, come to the Holy Church, come and receive the faith of Jesus Christ! " Padre Pieras could not help reminding his superior that not an Indian was within sight or hearing, and that it would be more practical to proceed with the ritual. One native, however, did witness the ceremony, and he soon brought a large number of his companions, who became

MISSION SAN CARLOS AND BAY OF MONTEREY.

Photograph by Howard Tibbitts, San Francisco.

JUNIPERO OAK, SAN CARLOS PRESIDIO MISSION, MONTEREY.

Photograph by George Wharton James.

STATUE OF SAN LUIS REY, AT PALA MISSION CHAPEL.

See page 246.

tractable enough to help in erecting the rude
church, barracks and houses with which the priests
and soldiers were compelled to be content in those
early days.

On September 8, Padres Somera and Cambon
founded the Mission of San Gabriel Arcángel,
originally about six miles from the present site.
Here, at first, the natives were inclined to be hostile, a large force under two chieftains appearing,
in order to prevent the priests from holding their
service. But at the elevation of a painting of the
Virgin, the opposition ceased, and the two chieftains threw their necklaces at the feet of the
Beautiful Queen. Still, a few wicked men can
undo in a short time the work of many good ones.
Padre Palou says that outrages by soldiers upon
the Indian women precipitated an attack upon
the Spaniards, especially upon two, at one of
whom the chieftain (whose wife had been out-
raged by the man) fired an arrow. Stopping it
with his shield, the soldier levelled his musket and
shot the injured husband dead. Ah! sadness of
it! The unbridled passions of men of the new race
already foreshadowed the death of the old race,
even while the good priests were seeking to elevate
and to Christianize them. This attack and con-
sequent disturbance delayed still longer the founding of San Buenaventura.

On his way south (for he had now decided to go
to Mexico), Serra founded, on September 1, 1772,
the Mission of San Luis Obispo de Tolosa. The

natives called the location Tixlini, and half a league away was a famous canyada in which Fages, some time previously, had killed a number of bears to provide meat for the starving people at Monterey. This act made the natives well disposed towards the priests in charge of the new Mission, and they helped to erect buildings, offered their children for baptism, and brought of their supply of food to the priests, whose stores were by no means abundant.

While these events were transpiring, Governor Portolá had returned to Lower California, and Lieutenant Fages was appointed commandant in his stead. This, it soon turned out, was a great mistake. Fages and Serra did not work well together, and, at the time of the founding of San Luis Obispo, relations between them were strained almost to breaking. Serra undoubtedly had just cause for complaint. The enthusiastic, impulsive missionary, desirous of furthering his important religious work, believed himself to be restrained by a cold-blooded, official-minded soldier, to whom routine was more important than the salvation of the Indians. Serra complained that Fages opened his letters and those of his fellow missionaries; that he supported his soldiers when their evil conduct rendered the work of the missionaries unavailing; that he interfered with the management of the stations and the punishment of neophytes, and devoted to his own uses the property and facilities of the Missions.

In the main, this complaint received attention from the Junta in Mexico. Fages was ultimately removed, and Rivera appointed governor in his place. More missionaries, money, and supplies were placed at Serra's disposal, and he was authorized to proceed to the establishment of the additional Missions which he had planned. He also obtained authority from the highest powers of the Church to administer the important sacrament of confirmation. This is a right generally conferred only upon a bishop and his superiors, but as California was so remote and the visits of the bishop so rare, it was deemed appropriate to grant this privilege to Serra.

Rejoicing and grateful, the earnest president sent Padres Fermin Francisco de Lasuen and Gregorio Amurrio, with six soldiers, to begin work at San Juan Capistrano. This occurred in August, 1775. On the thirtieth of the following October, work was begun, and everything seemed auspicious, when suddenly, as if God had ceased to smile upon them, terrible news came from San Diego. There, apparently, things had been going well. Sixty converts were baptized on October 3, and the priests rejoiced at the success of their efforts. But the Indians back in the mountains were alarmed and hostile. Who were these white-faced strangers causing their brother aborigines to kneel before a strange God? What was the meaning of that mystic ceremony of sprinkling with water? The demon of priestly jealousy was

awakened in the breasts of the *tingaivashes* —
the medicine-men — of the tribes about San
Diego, who arranged a fierce midnight attack
which should rid them forever of these foreign
conjurers, the men of the " bad medicine."

Exactly a month and a day after the baptism of
the sixty converts, at the dead of night, the
Mission buildings were fired and the eleven persons of Spanish blood were awakened by flames
and the yells of a horde of excited savages. A
fierce conflict ensued. Arrows were fired on the
one side, gun-shots on the other, while the flames
roared in accompaniment and lighted the scene.
Both Indians and Spaniards fell. The following
morning, when hostilities had ceased and the
enemy had withdrawn, the body of Padre Jayme
was discovered in the dry bed of a neighboring
creek, bruised from head to foot with blows from
stones and clubs, naked, and bearing eighteen
arrow-wounds.

The sad news was sent to Serra, and his words,
at hearing it, show the invincible missionary
spirit of the man: " God be thanked! Now the
soil is watered; now will the reduction of the
Dieguinos be complete! "

At San Juan Capistrano, however, the news
caused serious alarm. Work ceased, the bells were
buried, and the priests returned.

In the meantime events were shaping elsewhere
for the founding of the Mission of San Francisco.
Away yonder, in what is now Arizona, but was

then a part of New Mexico, were several Missions, some forty miles south of the city of Tucson, and it was decided to connect these, by means of a good road, with the Missions of California. Captain Juan Bautista de Anza was sent to find this road. He did so, and made the trip successfully, going with Padre Serra from San Gabriel as far north as Monterey.

On his return, the Viceroy, Bucareli, gave orders that he should recruit soldiers and settlers for the establishment and protection of the new Mission on San Francisco Bay. We have a full roster, in the handwriting of Padre Font, the Franciscan who accompanied the expedition, of those who composed it. Successfully they crossed the sandy wastes of Arizona and the barren desolation of the Colorado Desert (in Southern California).

On their arrival at San Gabriel, January 4, 1776 (memorable year on the other side of the continent), they found that Rivera, who had been appointed governor in Portolá's stead, had arrived the day before, on his way south to quell the Indian disturbances at San Diego, and Anza, on hearing the news, deemed the matter of sufficient importance to justify his turning aside from his direct purpose and going south with Rivera. Taking seventeen of his soldiers along, he left the others to recruit their energies at San Gabriel, but the inactivity of Rivera did not please him, and, as things were not going well at San Gabriel,

he soon returned and started northward. It was
a weary journey, the rains having made some parts
of the road well-nigh impassable, and even the
women had to walk. Yet on the tenth of March
they all arrived safely and happily at Monterey,
where Serra himself came to congratulate them.

After an illness which confined him to his bed,
Anza, against the advice of his physician, started
to investigate the San Francisco region, as upon
his decision rested the selection of the site. The
bay was pretty well explored, and the site chosen,
near a spring and creek, which was named from the
day, — the last Friday in Lent, — *Arroyo de los
Dolores*. Hence the name so often applied to the
Mission itself: it being commonly known even
to-day as " Mission Dolores."

His duty performed, Anza returned south, and
Rivera appointed Lieutenant Moraga to take
charge of the San Francisco colonists, and on
July 26, 1776, a camp was pitched on the
allotted site. The next day a building of tules
was begun and on the twenty-eighth of the same
month mass was said by Padre Palou. In the
meantime, the vessel " San Carlos " was expected
from Monterey with all needful supplies for both
the *presidio* and the new Mission, but, buffeted
by adverse winds, it was forced down the coast
as far as San Diego, and did not arrive outside
of what is now the bay of San Francisco until
August 17.

The two carpenters from' the " San Carlos,"

with a squad of sailors, were set to work on the new
buildings, and on September 17 the foundation ceremonies of the *presidio* took place. On that same
day, Lord Howe, of the British army, with his
Hessian mercenaries, was rejoicing in the city of
New York in anticipation of an easy conquest of
the army of the revolutionists.

It was the establishment of that *presidio*, followed by that of the Mission on October 9, which
predestined the name of the future great American
city, born of adventure and romance.

Padres Palou and Cambon had been hard at
work since the end of July. Aided by Lieutenant
Moraga, they built a church fifty-four feet long,
and a house thirty by fifteen feet, both structures
being of wood, plastered with clay, and roofed with
tules. On October 3, the day preceding the festival
of St. Francis, bunting and flags from the ships
were brought to decorate the new buildings; but,
owing to the absence of Moraga, the formal dedication did not take place until October 9. Happy
was Serra's friend and brother, Palou, to celebrate
high mass at this dedication of the church named
after the great founder of his Order, and none the
less so were his assistants, Fathers Cambon,
Nocedal, and Peña.

Just before the founding of the Mission of
San Francisco, the Spanish Fathers witnessed an
Indian battle. Natives advanced from the region
of San Mateo and vigorously attacked the San
Francisco Indians, burning their houses and com-

pelling them to flee on their tule rafts to the islands and the opposite shores of the bay. Months elapsed before these defeated Indians returned, to afford the Fathers at San Francisco an' opportunity to work for the salvation of their souls.

In October of the following year, Serra paid his first visit to San Francisco, and said mass on the titular saint's day. Then, standing near the Golden Gate, he exclaimed: " Thanks be to God that now our father, St. Francis, with the holy professional cross of Missions, has reached the last limit of the Californian continent. To go farther he must have boats."

The same month in which Palou dedicated the northern Mission, found Serra, with Padre Gregorio Amurrio and ten soldiers, wending their way from San Diego to San Juan Capistrano, the foundation of which had been delayed the year previous by the San Diego massacre. They disinterred the bells and other buried materials and without delay founded the Mission. With his customary zeal, Serra caused the bells to be hung and sounded, and said the dedicatory mass on November 1, 1776. The original location of this Mission, named by the Indians *Sajirit*, was approximately the site of the present church, whose pathetic ruins speak eloquently of the frightful earthquake which later destroyed it.

Aroused by a letter from Viceroy Bucareli, Rivera hastened the establishment of the eighth Mission. A place was found near the Guadalupe

River, where the Indians named *Tares* had four *rancherias*, and which they called *Thamien*. Here Padre Tomás de la Peña planted the cross, erected an *enramada*, or brush shelter, and on January 12, 1777, said mass, dedicating the new Mission to the Virgin, Santa Clara, one of the early converts of Francis of Assisi.

On February 3, 1777, the new governor of Alta California, Felipe de Neve, arrived at Monterey and superseded Rivera. He quickly established the pueblo of San José, and, a year or two later, Los Angeles, the latter under the long title of the pueblo of "Nuestra Señora, Reina de los Angeles," — Our Lady, Queen of the Angels.

In the meantime, contrary to the advice and experience of the padres, the new Viceroy, Croix, determined to establish two Missions on the Colorado River, near the site of the present city of Yuma, and conduct them not as Mission , with the Fathers exercising control over the Indians, but as towns in which the Indians would be under no temporal restraint. The attempt was unfortunate. The Indians fell upon the Spaniards and priests, settlers, soldiers, and Governor Rivera himself perished in the terrific attack. Forty-six men met an awful fate, and the women were left to a slavery more frightful than death. This was the last attempt made by the Spaniards to missionize the Yumas.

With these sad events in mind the Fathers founded San Buenaventura on March 31, 1782.

Serra himself preached the dedicatory sermon. The Indians came from their picturesque conical huts of tule and straw, to watch the raising of the cross, and the gathering at this dedication was larger than at any previous ceremony in California; more than seventy Spaniards with their families, together with large numbers of Indians, being there assembled.

The next month, the *presidio* of Santa Barbara was established.

In the end of 1783, Serra visited all the southern Missions to administer confirmation to the neophytes, and in January, 1784, he returned to San Carlos at Monterey.

For some time his health had been failing, asthma and a running sore on his breast both causing him much trouble. Everywhere uneasiness was felt at his physical condition, but though he undoubtedly suffered keenly, he refused to take medicine. The padres were prepared at any time to hear of his death. But Serra calmly went on with his work. He confirmed the neophytes at San Luis Obispo and San Antonio, and went to help dedicate the new church recently built at Santa Clara, and also to San Francisco. Called back to Santa Clara by the sickness of Padre Murguia, he was saddened by the death of that noble and good man, and felt he ought to prepare himself for death. But he found strength to return to San Carlos at Monterey, and there, on Saturday, August 28, 1784, he passed to his eternal reward, at the ripe age of seventy years, nine months and four days. His last act was to walk to the door, in order that he might look out upon the beautiful face of Nature. The ocean, the sky, the trees, the valley with its wealth of verdure, the birds, the flowers — all gave joy to his 'weary eyes. Returning to his bed, he " fell asleep," and his work on earth ended. He was buried by his friend Palou at his beloved Mission in the Carmelo Valley, and there his dust now rests.[1]

[1] In 1787 Padre Palou published, in the City of Mexico, his "Life and Apostolic Labors of the Venerable Padre Junipero Serra." This has never yet been translated, until this year, 1913, the bi-centenary of his birth, when I have had the work done by a competent scholar, revised by the eminent Franciscan historian, Father Zephyrin Englehardt, with annotations.   It is a work of over three hundred pages, and is an important contribution to the historic literature of California.

CHAPTER IV

THE MISSIONS FOUNDED BY PADRE FERMIN FRANCISCO LASUEN

At Padre Serra's death Fermin Francisco Lasuen was chosen to be his successor as padre-presidente. At the time of his appointment he was the priest in charge at San Diego. He was elected by the directorate of the Franciscan College of San Fernando, in the City of Mexico, February 6, 1785, and on March 13, 1787, the Sacred Congregation at Rome confirmed his appointment, according to him the same right of confirmation which Serra had exercised. In five years this Father confirmed no less than ten thousand, one hundred thirty-nine persons.

Santa Barbara was the next Mission to be founded. For awhile it seemed that it would be located at Montecito, now the beautiful and picturesque suburb of its larger sister; but President Lasuen doubtless chose the site the Mission now occupies. Well up on the foothills of the Sierra Santa Inés, it has a commanding view of valley, ocean and islands beyond. Indeed, for outlook, it is doubtful if any other Mission equals it. It was formally dedicated on **December 4, 1786.**

Various obstacles to the establishment of Santa Barbara had been placed in the way of the priests. Governor Fages wished to curtail their authority, and sought to make innovations which the padres regarded as detrimental in the highest degree to the Indians, as well as annoying and humiliating to themselves. This was the reason of the long delay in founding Santa Barbara. It was the same with the following Mission. It had long been decided upon. Its site was selected. The natives called it *Algsacupi.* It was to be dedicated "to the most pure and sacred mystery of the Immaculate Conception of the most Holy Virgin Mary, Mother of God, Queen of Heaven, Queen of Angels, and Our Lady," a name usually, however, shortened in Spanish parlance to " La Purísima Concepción." On December 8, 1787, Lasuen blessed the site, raised the cross, said mass and preached a sermon; but it was not until March, 1788, that work on the buildings was begun. An adobe structure, roofed with tiles, was completed in 1802, and, ten years later, destroyed by earthquake.

The next Mission founded by Lasuen was that of Santa Cruz. On crossing the coast range from Santa Clara, he thus wrote: " I found in the site the most excellent fitness which had been reported to me. I found, beside, a stream of water, very near, copious, and important. On August 28, the day of Saint Augustine, I said mass, and raised a cross on the spot where the establishment is to be.

Many gentiles came, old and young, of both sexes, and showed that they would gladly enlist under the Sacred Standard. Thanks be to God!"

On Sunday, September 25, Sugert, an Indian chief of the neighborhood, assured by the priests and soldiers that no harm should come to him or his people by the noise of exploding gunpowder, came to the formal founding. Mass was said, a *Te Deum* chanted, and Don Hermenegildo Sol, Commandant of San Francisco, took possession of the place, thus completing the foundation. To-day nothing but a memory remains of the Mission of the Holy Cross, it having fallen into ruins and totally disappeared.

Lasuen's fourth Mission was founded in this same year, 1791. He had chosen a site, called by the Indians *Chuttusgelis*, and always known to the Spaniards as Soledad, since their first occupation of the country. Here, on October 9, Lasuen, accompanied by Padres Sitjar and Garcia, in the presence of Lieutenant José Arguello, the guard, and a few natives, raised the cross, blessed the site, said mass, and formally established the Mission of "Nuestra Senyora de la Soledad."

One interesting entry in the Mission books is worthy of mention. In September, 1787, two vessels belonging to the newly founded United States sailed from Boston. The smaller of these was the "Lady Washington," under command of Captain Gray. In the Soledad Mission register of baptisms, it is written that on May 19, 1793, there was baptized a Nootka Indian, twenty years of age, " Inquina, son of a gentile father, named Taguasmiki, who in the year 1789 was killed by the American Gert [undoubtedly Gray], Captain of the vessel called ' Washington,' belonging to the Congress of Boston."

For six years no new Missions were founded: then, in 1797, four were established, and one in 1798. These, long contemplated, were delayed for a variety of reasons. It was the purpose of the Fathers to have the new Missions farther inland than those already established, that they might reach more of the natives: those who lived in the valleys and on the slopes of the foothills. Besides this, it had always been the intent of the Spanish government that further explorations of the interior country should take place, so that, as the Missions became strong enough to support themselves, the Indians there might be brought under the influence of the Church. Governor Neve's regulations say:

" It is made imperative to increase the number of Reductions (stations for converting the Indians) in proportion to the vastness of the country occupied, and although this must be carried out in the succession and order aforesaid, as fast as the older establishments shall be fully secure, etc.," and earlier, " while the breadth of the country is unknown (it) is presumed to be as great as the length, or greater (200 leagues), since its greatest breadth is counted by thousands of leagues."

Various investigations were made by the nearest priests in order to select the best locations for the proposed Missions, and, in 1796, Lasuen reported the results to the new governor, Borica, who in turn communicated them to the Viceroy in Mexico. Approval was given and orders issued for the establishment of the five new Missions.

On June 9, 1797, Lasuen left San Francisco for the founding of the Mission San José, then called the Alameda. The following day, a brush church was erected, and, on the morrow, the usual foundation ceremonies occurred. The natives named the site *Oroysom*. Beautifully situated on the foothills, with a prominent peak near by, it offers an extensive view over the southern portion of the San Francisco Bay region. At first, a wooden structure with a grass roof served as a church; but later a brick structure was erected, which Von Langsdorff visited in 1806.

It seems singular to us at this date that although the easiest means of communication between the Missions of Santa Clara, San José and San Francisco was by water on the Bay of San Francisco, the padre and soldiers at San Francisco had no boat or vessel of any kind. Langsdorff says of this: "Perhaps the missionaries are afraid lest if there were boats, they might facilitate the escape of the Indians, who never wholly lose their love of freedom and their attachment to their native habits; they therefore consider it better to confine their communication with one another to the means afforded by the land. The Spaniards, as well as their nurslings, the Indians, are very seldom under the necessity of trusting themselves to the waves, and if such a necessity occur, they make a kind of boat for the occasion, of straw, reeds, and rushes, bound together so closely as to be water-tight. In this way they contrive to go very easily from one shore to the other. Boats of this kind are called *walza* by the Spanish. The oars consist of a thin, long pole somewhat broader at each end, with which the occupants row sometimes on one side, sometimes on the other."

For the next Mission two sites were suggested; but, as early as June 17, Corporal Ballesteros erected a church, missionary-house, granary, and guard-house at the point called by the natives *Popeloutchom*, and by the Spaniards, San Benito. Eight days later, Lasuen, aided by Padres Catala and Martiarena, founded the Mission dedicated to the saint of that day, San Juan Bautista.

Next in order, between the two Missions of San Antonio de Padua and San Luis Obispo, was that of " the most glorious prince of the heavenly militia," San Miguel. Lasuen, aided by Sitjar, in the presence of a large number of Indians, performed the ceremony in the usual form, on July 25, 1797. This Mission eventually grew to large proportions and its interior remains to-day almost exactly as decorated by the hands of the original priests.

San Fernando Rey was next established, on September 8, by Lasuen, aided by Padre Dumetz.

After extended correspondence between Lasuen and Governor Borica, a site, called by the natives *Tacayme*, was finally chosen for locating the next Mission, which was to bear the name of San Luis, Rey de Francia. Thus it became necessary to distinguish between the two saints of the same name: San Luis, Bishop (Obispo), and San Luis, King; but modern American parlance has eliminated the comma, and they are respectively San Luis Obispo and San Luis Rey. Lasuen, with the honored Padre Peyri and Padre Santiago, conducted the ceremonies on June 13, and the hearts of all concerned were made glad by the subsequent baptism of fifty-four children.

It was as an adjunct to this Mission that Padre Peyri, in 1816, founded the chapel of San Antonio de Pala, twenty miles east from San Luis Rey: to which place were removed the Palatingwas, or Agua Calientes, evicted a few years ago from Warner's Ranch. This chapel has the picturesque *campanile*, or small detached belfry, the pictures of which are known throughout the world.

With the founding of San Luis Rey this branch of the work of President Lasuen terminated. Bancroft regards him as a greater man than Serra, and one whose life and work entitle him to the highest praise. He died at San Carlos on June 26, 1803, and was buried by the side of Serra.

CHAPTER V

THE FOUNDING OF SANTA INÉS, SAN RAFAEL AND SAN FRANCISCO SOLANO

ESTEVAN TAPIS now became president of the Missions, and under his direction was founded the nineteenth Mission, that of Santa Inés, virgin and martyr. Tapis himself conducted the ceremonies, preaching a sermon to a large congregation, including Commandant Carrillo, on September 17, 1804.

With Lasuen, the Mission work of California reached its maximum power. Under his immediate successors it began to decline. Doubtless the fact that the original chain was completed was an influence in the decrease of activity. For thirteen years there was no extension. A few minor attempts were made to explore the interior country, and many of the names now used for rivers and locations in the San Joaquin Valley were given at this time. Nothing further, however, was done, until in 1817, when such a wide-spread mortality affected the Indians at the San Francisco Mission, that Governor Sola suggested that the afflicted neophytes be removed to a new and healthful location on the north shore of the San

Francisco Bay. A few were taken to what is now San Rafael, and while some recovered, many died. These latter, not having received the last rites of religion, were subjects of great solicitude on the part of some of the priests, and, at last, Father Taboada, who had formerly been the priest at La Purísima Concepción, consented to take charge of this branch Mission. The native name of the site was *Nanaguani.* On December 14, Padre Sarría, assisted by several other priests, conducted the ceremony of dedication to San Rafael Arcángel. It was originally intended to be an *asistencia* of San Francisco, but although there is no record that it was ever formally raised to the dignity of an independent Mission, it is called and enumerated as such from the year 1823 in all the reports of the Fathers. To-day, not a brick of its walls remains; the only evidence of its existence being the few old pear trees planted early in its history.

There are those who contend that San Rafael was founded as a direct check to the southward aggressions of the Russians, who in 1812 had established Fort Ross, but sixty-five miles north of San Francisco. There seems, however, to be no recorded authority for this belief, although it may easily be understood how anxious this close proximity of the Russians made the Spanish authorities.

They had further causes of anxiety. The complications between Mexico and Spain, which

culminated in the independence of the former, and
then the establishment of the Empire, gave the
leaders enough to occupy their minds.

The final establishment took place in 1823,
without any idea of founding a new Mission. The
change to San Rafael had been so beneficial to
the sick Indians that Canon Fernandez, Prefect
Payeras, and Governor Argüello decided to
transfer bodily the Mission of San Francisco
from the peninsula to the mainland north of the
bay, and make San Rafael dependent upon it.
An exploring expedition was sent out which
somewhat carefully examined the whole neighborhood and finally reported in favor of the
Sonoma Valley. The report being accepted, on
July 4, 1823, a cross was set up and blessed on the
site, which was named New San Francisco.

Padre Altimira, one of the explorers, now wrote
to the new padre presidente — Señan — explaining
what he had done, and his reasons for so doing;
stating that San Francisco could no longer exist,
and that San Rafael was unable to subsist alone.
Discussion followed, and Sarría, the successor
of Señan, who had died, refused to authorize the
change; expressing himself astonished at the
audacity of those who had dared to take so important a step without consulting the supreme
government. Then Altimira, infuriated, wrote
to the governor, who had been a party to the
proposed removal, concluding his tirade by saying:
" I came to convert gentiles and to establish

new Missions, and if I cannot do it here, which, as we all agree, is the best spot in California for the purpose, I will leave the country."

Governor Argüello assisted his priestly friend as far as he was able, and apprised Sarría that he would sustain the new establishment; although he would withdraw the order for the suppression of San Rafael. A compromise was then effected by which New San Francisco was to remain a Mission in regular standing, but neither San Rafael nor old San Francisco were to be disturbed.

Is it not an inspiring subject for speculation? Where would the modern city of San Francisco be, if the irate Father and plotting politicians of those early days had been successful in their schemes?

The new Mission, all controversy being settled, was formally dedicated on Passion Sunday, April 4, 1824, by Altimira, to San Francisco Solano, " the great apostle to the Indies." There were now two San Franciscos, de Asis and Solano, and because of the inconvenience arising from this confusion, the popular names, Dolores and Solano, and later, Sonoma, came into use.

From the point now reached, the history of the Missions is one of distress, anxiety, and final disaster. Their great work was practically ended.

CHAPTER VI

It is generally believed that the California Indian in his original condition was one of the most miserable and wretched of the world's aborigines. As one writer puts it:

"When discovered by the padres he was almost naked, half starved, living in filthy little hovels built of tule, speaking a meagre language broken up into as many different and independent dialects as there were tribes, having no laws and few definite customs, cruel, simple, lazy, and — in one word which best describes such a condition of existence — wretched. There are some forms of savage life that we can admire; there are others that can only excite our disgust; of the latter were the California Indians."

This is the general attitude taken by most writers of this later day, as well as of the padres themselves, yet I think I shall be able to show that in some regards it is a mistaken one. I do not believe the Indians were the degraded and brutal creatures the padres and others have endeavored to make out. This is no charge of bad faith against these writers. It is merely a criticism of their judgment.

The fact that in a few years the Indians became remarkably competent in so many fields of skilled labor is the best answer to the unfounded charges of abject savagery. Peoples are not civilized nor educated in a day. Brains cannot be put into a monkey, no matter how well educated his teacher is. There must have been the mental quality, the ability to learn; or even the miraculous patience, perseverance, and love of the missionaries would not have availed to teach them, in several hundred years, much less, then, in the half-century they had them under their control, the many things we know they learned.

The Indians, prior to the coming of the padres, were skilled in some arts, as the making of pottery, basketry, canoes, stone axes, arrow heads, spear heads, stone knives, and the like. Holder says of the inhabitants of Santa Catalina that although their implements were of stone, wood, or shell " the skill with which they modelled and made their weapons, mortars, and steatite *ollas,* their rude mosaics of abalone shells, and their manufacture of pipes, medicine-tubes, and flutes give them high rank among savages." The mortars found throughout California, some of which are now to be seen in the museums of Santa Barbara, Los Angeles, San Diego, etc., are models in shape and finish. As for their basketry, I have elsewhere [1] shown that it alone stamps them as an

[1] Indian Basketry, especially the chapters on Form, Poetry, and Symbolism.

artistic, mechanically skilful, and mathematically inclined people, and the study of their designs and their meanings reveal a love of nature, poetry, sentiment, and religion that put them upon a superior plane.

Cabrillo was the first white man so far as we know who visited the Indians of the coast of California. He made his memorable journey in 1542-1543. In 1539, Ulloa sailed up the Gulf of California, and, a year later, Alarcon and Diaz explored the Colorado River, possibly to the point where Yuma now stands. These three men came in contact with the Cocopahs and the Yumas, and possibly with other tribes.

Cabrillo tells of the Indians with whom he held communication. They were timid and somewhat hostile at first, but easily appeased. Some of them, especially those living on the islands (now known as San Clemente, Santa Catalina, Anacapa, Santa Barbara, Santa Rosa, San Miguel, and Santa Cruz), were superior to those found inland. They rowed in pine canoes having a seating capacity of twelve or thirteen men, and were expert fishermen. They dressed in the skins of animals, were rude agriculturists, and built for themselves shelters or huts of willows, tules, and mud.

The principal written source of authority for our knowledge of the Indians at the time of the arrival of the Fathers is Fray Geronimo Boscana's *Chinigchinich: A Historical Account*, etc.,

of the Indians of San Juan Capistrano. There
are many interesting things in this account, some
of importance, and others of very slight value.
He insists that there was a great difference in the
intelligence of the natives north of Santa Barbara
and those to the south, in favor of the former.
Of these he says they " are much more industrious,
and appear an entirely distinct race. They formed,
from shells, a kind of money, which passed current
among them, and they constructed)ut of logs
very swift and excellent canoes for fishing."

Of the character of his Indians he had a very
poor idea. He compares them to 'monkeys who
imitate, and especially in their copying the ways
of the white men, " whom they respect as beings
much superior to themselves; but in so doing,
they are careful to select vice in preference to
virtue. This is the result, undoubtedly, of their
corrupt and natural disposition."

Of the language of the California Indians, Boscana says there was great diversity, finding a
new dialect almost every fifteen to twenty leagues.

They were not remarkably industrious, yet
the men made their home utensils, bows and
arrows, the several instruments used in making
baskets, and also constructed nets, spinning the
thread from yucca fibres, which they beat and
prepared for that purpose. They also built the
'ouses.

The women gathered seeds, prepared them, and
did the cooking, as well as all the household duties.

They made the baskets, all other utensils being made by the men.

The dress of the men, when they dressed at all, consisted of the skins of animals thrown over the shoulders, leaving the rest of the body exposed, but the women wore a cloak and dress of twisted rabbit-skins. I have found these same rabbit-skin dresses in use by Mohave and Yumas within the past three or four years.

The youths were required to keep away from the fire, in order that they might learn to suffer with bravery and courage. They were forbidden also to eat certain kinds of foods, to teach them to bear deprivation and to learn to control their appetites. In addition to these there were certain ceremonies, which included fasting, abstinence from drinking, and the production of hallucinations by means of a vegetable drug, called pivat (still used, by the way, by some of the Indians of Southern California), and the final branding of the neophyte, which Boscana describes as follows: " A kind of herb was pounded until it became sponge-like; this they placed, according to the figure required, upon the spot intended to be burnt, which was generally upon the right arm, and sometimes upon the thick part of the leg also. They then set fire to it, and let it remain until all that was combustible was consumed. Consequently, a large blister immediately formed, and although painful, they used no remedy to cure it, but left it to heal itself; and thus, a large and perpetual scar remained. The reason alleged for this ceremony was that it added greater strength to the nerves, and gave a better pulse for the management of the bow." This ceremony was called *potense*.

The education of the girls was by no means neglected.

" They were taught to remain at home, and not to roam about in idleness; to be always employed in some domestic duty, so that, when they were older, they might know how to work, and attend to their household duties; such as procuring seeds, and cleaning them — making ' atole ' and ' pinole,' which are kinds of gruel, and their daily food. When quite young, they have a small, shallow basket, called by the natives ' tucmel,' with which they learn the way to clean the seeds, and they are also instructed in grinding, and preparing the same for consumption."

When a girl was married, her father gave her good advice as to her conduct. She must be faithful to her wifely duties and do nothing to disgrace either her husband or her parents. Children of tender years were sometimes betrothed by their parents. Padre Boscana says he married a couple, the girl having been but eight or nine months old, and the boy two years, when they were contracted for by their parents.

Childbirth was natural and easy with them, as it generally is with all primitive peoples. An Indian woman has been known to give birth to a child, walk half a mile to a stream, step into it and wash both herself and the new-born babe, then return to her camp, put her child in a *yakia*, or basket cradle-carrier, sling it over her back, and start on a four or five mile journey, on foot, up the rocky and steep sides of a canyon.

A singular custom prevailed among these people, not uncommon elsewhere. The men, when their wives were suffering their accouchement, would abstain from all flesh and fish, refrain from smoking and all diversions, and stay within the *Kish*, or hut, from fifteen to twenty days.

The god of the San Juan Indians was Chinig-chinich, and it is possible, from similarity in the ways of appearing and disappearing, that he is the monster Tauguitch of the Sabobas and Cahuillas described in The Legend of Tauguitch and Algoot.[1] This god was a queer compound of goodness and evil, who taught them all the rites and ceremonies that they afterwards observed.

Many of the men and a few women posed as possessing supernatural powers — witches, in fact, and such was the belief in their power that, " without resistance, all immediately acquiesce in their demands." They also had physicians who used cold water, plasters of herbs, whipping with nettles (doubtless the principle of the counter irritant), the smoke of certain plants, and incantations, with a great deal of general, all-around humbug to produce their cures.

But not all the medicine ideas and methods of

[1] See Folk Lore Journal, 1904.

the Indians were to be classed as humbug. **Dr. Cephas L.** Bard, who, besides extolling their temescals, or sweat-baths, their surgical abilities, as displayed in the operations that were performed upon skulls that have since been exhumed; their hygienic customs, which he declares " are not only commendable, but worthy of the consideration of an advanced civilization," states further:

" It has been reserved for the California Indian to furnish three of the most valuable vegetable additions which have been made to the Pharmacopœia during the last twenty years. One, the Eriodictyon Glutinosum, growing profusely in our foothills, was used by them in affections of the respiratory tract, and its worth was so appreciated by the Missionaries as to be named Yerba Santa, or Holy Plant. The second, the Rhamnus purshiana, gathered now for the market in the upper portions of the State, is found scattered through the timbered mountains of Southern California. It was used as a laxative, and on account of the constipating effect of an acorn diet, was doubtless in active demand. So highly was it esteemed by the followers of the Cross that it was christened Cascara Sagrada, or Sacred Bark. The third, Grindelia robusta, was used in the treatment of pulmonary troubles, and externally in poisoning from Rhus toxicodendron, or Poison Oak, and in various skin diseases."

Their food was of the crudest and simplest character. Whatever they could catch they ate, from deer or bear to grasshoppers, lizards, rats, and snakes. In baskets of their own manufacture, they gathered all kinds of wild seeds, and after using a rude process of threshing, they winnowed them. They also gathered mesquite beans in large quantities, burying them in pits for a month or two, in order to extract from them certain disagreeable flavors, and then storing them in large and rudely made willow granaries. But, as Dr. Bard well says:

" Of the Vegetable articles of diet the acorn was the principal one. It was deprived of its bitter taste by grinding, running through sieves made of interwoven grasses, and frequent washings. Another one was Chia, the seeds of Salvia Columbariae, which in appearance are somewhat similar to birdseed. They were roasted, ground, and used as a food by being mixed with water. Thus prepared, it soon develops into a mucilaginous mass, larger than its original bulk. Its taste is somewhat like that of linseed meal. It is exceedingly nutritious, and was readily borne by the stomach when that organ refused to tolerate other aliment. An atole, or gruel, of this was one of the peace offerings to the first visiting sailors. One tablespoonful of these seeds was sufficient to sustain for twenty-four hours an Indian on a forced march. Chia was no less prized by the native Californian, and at this late date it frequently commands $6 or $8 a pound.

" The pinion, the fruit of the pine, was largely used, and until now annual expeditions are made by the few surviving members of the coast tribes to the mountains for a supply. That they cultivated maize in certain localities, there can be but little doubt. They intimated to Cabrillo by signs that such was the case, and the supposition is confirmed by the presence at various points of vestiges of irrigating ditches. Yslay, the fruit of the wild cherry, was used as a food, and prepared by fermentation as an intoxicant. The seeds, ground and made into balls, were esteemed highly. The fruit of the manzanita, the seeds of burr clover, malva, and alfileri, were also used. Tunas, the fruit of the cactus, and wild blackberries, existed in abundance, and were much relished. A sugar was extracted from a certain reed of the tulares."

Acorns, seeds, mesquite beans, and dried meat were all pounded up in a well made granite mortar, on the top of which, oftentimes, a basket hopper was fixed by means of pine gum. Some of these mortars were hewn from steatite, or soapstone, others from a rough basic rock, and many of them were exceedingly well made and finely shaped; results requiring much patience and no small artistic skill. Oftentimes these mortars were made in the solid granite rocks or boulders, found near the harvesting and winnowing places, and I have photographed many such during late years.

These Indians were polygamists, but much of what the missionaries and others have called their obscenities and vile conversations, were the simple and unconscious utterances of men and women whose instincts were not perverted. It is the invariable testimony of all careful observers of every class that as a rule the aborigines were healthy, vigorous, virile, and chaste, until they became demoralized by the whites. With many of them certain ceremonies had a distinct flavor of sex worship: a rude phallicism which exists to the present day. To the priests, as to most modern observers, these rites were offensive and obscene, but to the Indians they were only natural and simple prayers for the fruitfulness of their wives and of the other producing forces.

J. S. Hittell says of the Indians of California:

" They had no religion, no conception of a deity, or of a future life, no idols, no form of worship, no priests, no philosophical conceptions, no historical traditions, no proverbs, no mode of recording thought before the coming of the missionaries among them."

Seldom has there been so much absolute misstatement as in this quotation. Jeremiah Curtin, a life-long student of the Indian, speaking of the same Indians, makes a remark which applies with force to these statements:

" The Indian, *at every step*, stood face to face with divinity as he knew or understood it. He could never escape from the presence of those powers who had made the first world. . . . The most important question of all in Indian life was communication with divinity, intercourse with the spirits of divine personages."

In his *Creation Myths of Primitive America*, this studious author gives the names of a number of divinities, and the legends connected with them. He affirms positively that

" the most striking thing in all savage belief is the low estimate put upon man, when unaided by divine, uncreated power.   In Indian belief every object in the universe is divine except man! "

As to their having no priests, no forms of worship, no philosophical conceptions, no historical traditions, no proverbs, any one interested in the Indian of to-day knows that these things are untrue.   Whence came all the myths and legends that recent writers have gathered, a score of which I myself hold still unpublished in my notebook?   Were they all imagined after the arrival of the Mission Fathers?   By no means!   They have been handed down for countless centuries, and they come to us, perhaps a little corrupted, but still just as accurate as do the songs of Homer.

Every tribe had its medicine men, who were developed by a most rigorous series of tests; such as would dismay many a white man.   As to their philosophical conceptions and traditions, Curtin well says that in them

" we have a monument of thought which is absolutely unequalled, altogether unique in human experience. The special value of this thought lies, moreover, in the fact that it is primitive ; that it is the thought of ages long anterior to those which we find recorded in the eastern hemisphere, either in sacred books, in histories, or in literature, whether preserved on baked brick, burnt cylinders, or papyrus."

And if we go to the Pueblo Indians, the Nava-hos, the Pimas, and others, all of whom were brought more or less under the influence of the Franciscans, we find a mass of beliefs, deities, traditions, conceptions, and proverbs, which would overpower Mr. Hittell merely to collate.

Therefore, let it be distinctly understood that the Indian was not the thoughtless, unimaginative, irreligious, brutal savage which he is too often represented to be. He thought, and thought well, but still originally. He was religious, profoundly and powerfully so, but in his own way; he was a philosopher, but not according to Hittell; he was a worshipper, but not after the method of Serra, Palou, and their priestly coadjutors.

CHAPTER VII

THE INDIANS UNDER THE PADRES

THE first consideration of the padres in dealing with the Indians was the salvation of their souls. Of this no honest and honorable man can hold any question. Serra and his coadjutors believed, without equivocation or reserve, the doctrines of the Church. As one reads his diary, his thought on this matter is transparent. In one place he thus naïvely writes: " It seemed to me that they (the Indians) would fall shortly into the apostolic and evangelic net."

This accomplished, the Indians must be kept Christians, educated and civilized. Here is the crucial point. In reading criticisms upon the Mission system of dealing with the Indians, one constantly meets with such passages as the following: " The fatal defect of this whole Spanish system was that no effort was made to educate the Indians, or teach them to read, and think, and act for themselves."

To me this kind of criticism is both unjust and puerile. What is education? What is civilization?

Expert opinions as to these matters vary considerably, and it is in the very nature of men that they should vary. The Catholics had their ideas and they sought to carry them out with care and fidelity. How far they succeeded it is for the unprejudiced historians and philosophers of the future to determine. Personally, I regard the education given by the padres as eminently practical, even though I materially differ from them as to some of the things they regarded as religious essentials. Yet in honor it must be said that if I, or the Church to which I belong, or you and the Church to which you belong, reader, had been in California in those early days, your religious teaching or mine would have been entitled, justly, to as much criticism and censure as have ever been visited upon that of the padres. They did the best they knew, and, as I shall soon show, they did wonderfully well, far better than the enlightened government to which we belong has ever done. Certain essentials stood out before them. These were, to see that the Indians were baptized, taught the ritual of the Church, lived as nearly as possible according to the rules laid down for them, attended the services regularly, did their proper quota of work, were faithful husbands and wives and dutiful children. Feeling that they were indeed fathers of a race of children, the priests required obedience and work, as the father of any well-regulated American household does. And as a rule these " children," though occasionally rebellious, were willingly obedient.

Under this régime it is unquestionably true that the lot of the Indians was immeasurably improved from that of their aboriginal condition. They were kept in a state of reasonable cleanliness, were well clothed, were taught and required to do useful work, learned many new and helpful arts, and were instructed in the elemental matters of the Catholic faith. All these things were a direct advance.

It should not be overlooked, however, that the Spanish government provided skilled laborers from Spain or Mexico, and paid their hire, for the purpose of aiding the settlers in the various pueblos that were established. Master mechanics, carpenters, blacksmiths, and stone masons are mentioned in Governor Neve's Rules and Regulations, and it is possible that some of the Indians were taught by these skilled artisans. Under the guidance of the padres some of them were taught how to weave. Cotton was both grown and imported, and all the processes of converting it, and wool also, into cloth, were undertaken with skill and knowledge.

At San Juan Capistrano the swing and thud of the loom were constantly heard, there having been at one time as many as forty weavers all engaged at once in this useful occupation.

San Gabriel and San Luis Rey also had many expert weavers.

At all the Missions the girls and women, as well as the men, had their share in the general education. They had always been seed gatherers, grinders, and preparers of the food, and now they were taught the civilized methods of doing these things. Many became tailors as well as weavers; others learned to dye the made fabrics, as in the past they had dyed their basketry splints; and still others — indeed nearly all — became skilled in the delicate art of lace-making and drawn-work. They were natural adepts at fine embroidery, as soon as the use of the needle and colored threads was shown them, and some exquisite work is still preserved that they accomplished in this field. As candy-makers they soon became expert and manifested judicious taste.

To return to the men. Many of them became herders of cattle, horses and sheep, teamsters, and butchers. At San Gabriel alone a hundred cattle were slaughtered every Saturday as food for the Indians themselves. The hides of all slain animals were carefully preserved, and either tanned for home use or shipped East. Dana in *Two Years Before the Mast* gives interesting pictures of hide-shipping at San Juan Capistrano. A good tanner is a skilled laborer, and these Indians were not only expert makers of dressed leather, but they tanned skins and peltries with the hair or fur on. Indeed I know of many wonderful birds' skins, dressed with the feathers on, that are still in perfect preservation. As workers in leather they have never been surpassed. Many saddles, bridles, etc., were needed for Mission use, and as the ranches grew in numbers, they created a large market. It must be remembered that horseback riding was the chief method of travel in California for over a hundred years. Their carved leather work is still the wonder of the world. In the striking character of their designs, in the remarkable adaptation of the design, in its general shape and contour, to the peculiar form of the object to be decorated, — a stirrup, a saddle, a belt, etc., — and in the digital and manual dexterity demanded by its execution, nothing is left to be desired. Equally skilful were they in taking the horn of an ox or mountain sheep, heating it, and then shaping it into a drinking-cup, a spoon, or a ladle, and carving upon it designs that equal those found upon the pottery of the ancient world.

Shoemaking was extensively carried on, for sale on the ranches and to the trading-vessels. Tallow was tried out by the ton and run into underground brick vaults, some of which would hold in one mass several complete ship-loads. This was quarried out and then hauled to San Pedro, or the nearest port, for shipment. Sometimes it was run into great bags made of hides, that would hold from five hundred to a thousand pounds each, and then shipped.

Many of the Indians became expert carpenters, and a few even might be classed as fair cabinet-makers. There were wheelwrights and cart-makers who made the " carretas " that are now the joy of the relic-hunter. These were clumsy oxcarts, with wheels made of blocks, sawed or chopped off from the end of a large round log; a big hole was then bored, chiseled, or burned through its center, enabling it to turn on a rude wooden axle. Soap or tallow was sometimes used as a lubricant. This was the only wheeled conveyance in California as late as 1840. Other Indians did the woodwork in buildings, made fences, etc. Some were carvers, and there are not a few specimens of their work that will bear comparison with the work of far more pretentious artisans.

Many of them became blacksmiths and learned to work well in iron. In the Coronel Collection in the Los Angeles Chamber of Commerce are many specimens of the ironwork of the San Fernando neophytes. The work of this Mission was long and favorably known as that of superior artisans. The collection includes plough-points, anvils, bells, hoes, chains, locks and keys, spurs, hinges, scissors, cattle-brands, and other articles of use in the Mission communities. There are also fine specimens of hammered copper, showing their ability in this branch of the craftsman's art. As there was no coal at this time in California, these metal-workers all became charcoal-burners.

Bricks of adobe and also burned bricks and tiles were made at every Mission, I believe, and in later years tiles were made for sale for the houses of the more pretentious inhabitants of the pueblos. As lime and cement were needed, the Indians were taught how to burn the lime of the country, and the cement work then done remains to this day as solid as when it was first put down.

Many of them became expert bricklayers and stone-masons and cutters, as such work as that found at San Luis Rey, San Juan Capistrano, San Carlos, Santa Inés, and other Missions most eloquently testifies.

It is claimed that much of the distemper painting upon the church walls was done by the Indians, though surely it would be far easier to believe that the Fathers did it than they. For with their training in natural design, as shown in their exquisite baskets, and the work they accomplished in leather carving, I do not hesitate to say that mural decorations would have been far more artistic in design, more harmonious in color, and more skilfully executed if the Indians had been left to their own native ability.

A few became silversmiths, though none ever accomplished much in this line. They made better sandal-makers, shoemakers, and hatters. As horse-trainers they were speedily most efficient, the cunning of their minds finding a natural outlet in gaining supremacy over the lower animal. They braided their own riatas from rawhide, and soon surpassed their teachers in the use of them. They were fearless hunters with them, often " roping " the mountain lion and even going so far as to capture the dangerous grizzly bears with no other "weapon," and bring them down from the mountains for their bear and bull fights. As vaqueros, or cowboys, they were a distinct class. As daring riders as the world has ever seen, they instinctively knew the arts of herding cattle and sheep, and soon had that whole field of work in their keeping. "H. H.," in *Ramona*, has told what skilled sheep-shearers they were, and there are Indian bands to-day in Southern California whose services are eagerly sought at good wages because of their thoroughness, skill and rapidity.

Now, with this list of achievements, who shall say they were not educated? Something more than lack of education must be looked for as the reason for the degradation and disappearance of the Indian, and in the next chapter I think I can supply that missing reason.

At the end of sixty years, more than thirty thousand Indian converts lodged in the Mission buildings, under the direct and immediate guidance of the Fathers, and performed their allotted daily labors with cheerfulness and thoroughness. There were some exceptions necessarily, but in the main the domination of the missionaries was complete.

It has often been asked: "What became of all the proceeds of the work of the Mission Indians? Did the padres claim it personally? Was it sent to the mother house in Mexico?" etc. These questions naturally enter the minds of those who have read the criticisms of such writers as Wilson, Guinn, and Scanland. In regard to the missionaries, they were under a vow of poverty. As to the mother house, it is asserted on honor that up to 1838 not even as much as a *curio* had been sent there. After that, as is well known, there was nothing to send. The fact is, the proceeds all went into the Indian Community Fund for the benefit of the Indians, or the improvement of their Mission church, gardens, or workshops. The most careful investigations by experts have led to but one opinion, and that is that in the early days there was little or no foundation for the charge that the padres were accumulating money. During the revolution it is well known that the Missions practically supported the military for a number of years, even though the padres, their wards, and their churches all suffered in consequence.

CHAPTER VIII

THE SECULARIZATION OF THE MISSIONS

IT was not the policy or intention of the Government of Spain to found Missions in the New World solely for the benefit of the natives. Philanthropic motives doubtless influenced the rulers to a certain degree; but to civilize barbarous peoples and convert them to the Catholic faith meant not only the rescue of savages from future perdition, but the enlargement of the borders of the Church, the preparation for future colonization, and, consequently, the extension of Spanish power and territory.

At the very inception of the Missions this was the complex end in view; but the padres who were commissioned to initiate these enterprises were, almost without exception, consecrated to one work only, — the salvation of souls.

In the course of time this inevitably led to differences of opinion between the missionaries and the secular authorities in regard to the wisest methods of procedure. In spite of the arguments of the padres, these conflicts resulted in the secularization of some of the Missions prior to the founding of those in California; but the condition

of the Indians on the Pacific Coast led the padres
to believe that secularization was a result possible
only in a remote future. They fully understood
that the Missions were not intended to become
permanent institutions, yet faced the problem
of converting a savage race into christianized
self-supporting civilians loyal to the Spanish
Crown, — a problem which presented perplexities
and difficulties neither understood nor appreciated at the time by the government authorities
in Spain or Mexico, nor by the mass of critics
of the padres in our own day.

Whatever may have been the mental capacity,
ability, and moral status of the Indians from one
point of view, it is certain that the padres regarded
them as ignorant, vile, incapable, and totally lost
without the restraining and educating influences
of the Church. As year after year opened up the
complexities of the situation, the padres became
more and more convinced that it would require
an indefinite period of time to develop these un-
tamed children into law-abiding citizens, according to the standard of the white aggressors upon
their territory.

On the other hand, aside from envy, jealousy,
and greed, there were reasons why some of the
men in authority honestly believed a change in
the Mission system of administration would be
advantageous to the natives, the Church, and
the State.

There is a good as well as an evil side to the

great subject of " secularization." In England the word used is " disestablishment." In the United States, to-day, for our own government, the general sentiment of most of its inhabitants is in favor of what is meant by " secularization," though of course in many particulars the cases are quite different. In other words, it means the freedom of the Church from the control or help of the State. In such an important matter there is bound to be great diversity of opinion. Naturally, the church that is " disestablished " will be a most bitter opponent of the plan, as was the Church in Ireland, in Scotland, and in Wales. In England the " dissenters " — as all the members of the nonconformist churches are entitled — are practically unanimous for the disestablishment of the State or Episcopal Church, while the Episcopalians believe that such an act would " provoke the wrath of God upon the country wicked enough to perpetrate it." The same conflict — in a slightly different field — is that being waged in the United States to-day against giving aid to any church in its work of educating either white children or Indians in its own sectarian institutions. All the leading churches of the country have, I believe, at some time or other in their history, been willing to receive, and actually have received, government aid in the caring for and education of Indians. To-day it is a generally accepted policy that no such help shall be given.

But the question at issue is: Was the secularization of the Missions by Mexico a wise, just, and humane measure at the time of its adoption? Let the following history tell.

From the founding of the San Diego Mission in 1769, until about sixty years later, the padres were practically in undisturbed possession, administering affairs in accordance with the instructions issued by the viceroys and the mother house of Mexico.

In 1787 Inspector Sola claimed that the Indians were then ready for secularization; and if there be any honor connected with the plan eventually followed, it practically belongs to him. For, though none of his recommendations were accepted, he suggested the overthrow of the old methods for others which were somewhat of the same character as those carried out many years later.

In 1793 Viceroy Gigedo referred to the secularization of certain Missions which had taken place in Mexico, and expressed his dissatisfaction with the results. Three years later, Governor Borica, writing on the same subject, expressed his opinion with force and emphasis, as to the length of time it would take to prepare the California Indians for citizenship. He said: "Those of New California, at the rate they are advancing, will not reach the goal in ten centuries; the reason God knows, and men know something about it."

In 1813 came the first direct attack upon the Mission system from the Cortes in Spain. Prior to this time a bishop had been appointed to have charge over church affairs in California, but there were too few parish churches, and he had too few clergy to send to such a far-away field to think of disturbing the present system for the Indians. But on September 13, 1813, the Cortes passed a decree that all the Missions in America that had been founded ten years should at once be given up to the bishop "without excuse or pretext whatever, in accordance with the laws." The Mission Fathers in charge might be appointed as temporary curates, but, of course, under the control of the bishop instead of the Mission president as hitherto. This decree, for some reason, was not officially published or known in California for seven or eight years; but when, on January 20, 1821, Viceroy Venadito did publish the royal confirmation of the decree, the guardian of the college in Mexico ordered the president of the California Missions to comply at once with its requirements. He was to surrender all property, but to exact a full inventoried receipt, and he was to notify the bishop that the missionaries were ready to surrender their charges to their successors. In accordance with this order, President Payeras notified Governor Sola of his readiness to give up the Missions, and rejoiced in the opportunity it afforded his co-workers to engage in new spiritual conquests among the heathen. But this was a false alarm. The bishop responded that the decree had not been enforced elsewhere, and as for him the California padres might remain at their posts. Governor Sola said he had received no official news of so important a change, but that when he did he " would act with the circumspection and prudence which so delicate a subject demands."

With Iturbide's imperial regency came a new trouble to California, largely provoked by thoughts of the great wealth of the Missions. The imperial decree creating the regency was not announced until the end of 1821, and practically all California acquiesced in it. But in the meantime Agustin Fernandez de San Vicente had been sent as a special commissioner to " learn the feelings of the Californians, to foment a spirit of independence, to obtain an oath of allegiance, to raise the new national flag," and in general to superintend the change of government. He arrived in Monterey September 26, but found nothing to alarm him, as nobody seemed to care much which way things went. Then followed the " election " of a new governor, and the wire-pullers announced that Luis Argüello was the " choice of the convention."

In 1825 the Mexican republic may be said to have become fairly well established. Iturbide was out of the way, and the politicians were beginning to rule. A new " political chief " was now sent to California in the person of José María Echeandía, who arrived in San Diego late in October, 1825. While he and his superiors in

Mexico were desirous of bringing about secularization, the difficulties in the way seemed insurmountable. The Missions were practically the backbone of the country; without them all would crumble to pieces, and the most fanatical opponent of the system could not fail to see that without the padres it would immediately fall. As Clinch well puts it: "The converts raised seven eighths of the farm produce; — the Missions had gathered two hundred thousand bushels in a single harvest. All manufacturing in the province — weaving, tanning, leather-work, flour-mills, soap-making — was carried on exclusively by the pupils of the Franciscans. It was moie than doubtful whether they could be got to work under any other management, and a sudden cessation of labor might ruin the whole territory."

Something must be done, so, after consultation with some of the more advanced of the padres, the governor issued a proclamation July 25, 1826, announcing to the Indians that those who desired to leave the Missions might do so, provided they had been Christians from childhood, or for fifteen years, were married, or at least not minors, and had some means of gaining a livelihood. The Indians must apply to the commandant at the presidio, who, after obtaining from the padre a report, was to issue a written permit entitling the neophyte and his family to go where they chose, their names being erased from the Mission register.

The result of this might readily be foreseen. Few could take advantage of it, and those that did soon came in contact with vultures of the " superior race," who proceeded to devour them and their substance.

Between July 29 and August 3, 1830, Echeandía had the California *diputacion* discuss his fuller plans, which they finally approved. These provided for the gradual transformation of the Missions into pueblos, beginning with those nearest the presidios and pueblos, of which one or two were to be secularized within a year, and the rest as rapidly as experience proved practicable. Each neophyte was to have a share in the Mission lands and other property. The padres might remain as curates, or establish a new line of Missions among the hitherto unreached Indians as they should choose. Though this plan was passed, it was not intended that it should be carried out until approved by the general government of Mexico.

All this seems singular to us now, reading three quarters of a century later, for, March 8, 1830, Manuel Victoria was appointed political chief in Echeandía's stead; but as he did not reach San Diego until November or December, and in the meantime a new element had been introduced into the secularization question in the person of José María Padrés, Echeandía resolved upon a bold stroke. He delayed meeting Victoria, lured him up to Santa Barbara, and kept him there under various pretexts until he had had time to prepare and issue a decree. This was dated January 6, 1831. It was a political trick, " wholly illegal, uncalled for, and unwise." He decreed immediate secularization of all the Missions, and the turning into towns of Carmel and San Gabriel. The ayuntamiento of Monterey, in accordance with the decree, chose a commissioner for each of the seven Missions of the district. These were Juan B. Alvarado for San Luis Obispo, José Castro for San Miguel, Antonio Castro for San Antonio, Tiburcio Castro for Soledad, Juan Higuera for San Juan Bautista, Sebastian Rodriguez for Santa Cruz, and Manuel Crespo for San Carlos. Castro and Alvarado were sent to San Miguel and San Luis Obispo respectively, where they read the decree and made speeches to the Indians; at San Miguel, Alvarado made a spread-eagle speech from a cart and used all his eloquence to persuade the Indians to adopt the plan of free-men. " Henceforth their trials were to be over. No tyrannical priest could compel them to work. They were to be citizens in a free and glorious republic, with none to molest or make them afraid." Then he called for those who wished to enjoy these blessings of freedom to come to the right, while those who were content to remain under the hideous bondage of the Missions could go to the left. Imagine his surprise and the chill his oratory received when all but a small handful quickly went to the left, and those who at first went to the right speedily joined the majority. At San Luis and San Antonio the Indians also preferred " slavery."

By this time Victoria began to see that he was being played with, so he hurried to Monterey and demanded the immediate surrender of the office to which he was entitled. One of his first acts was to nullify Echeandía's decree, and to write to Mexico and explain fully that it was undoubtedly owing to the influence of Padrés, whom he well knew. But before the end of the year Echeandía and his friends rose in rebellion, deposed, and exiled Victoria. Owing to the struggles then going on in Mexico, which culminated in Santa Anna's dictatorship, the revolt of Echeandía was overlooked and Figueroa appointed governor in his stead.

For a time Figueroa held back the tide of secularization, while Carlos Carrillo, the Californian delegate to the Mexican Congress, was doing all he could to keep the Missions and the Pious Fund intact. Figueroa then issued a series of provisional regulations on gradual emancipation, hoping to be relieved from further responsibility by the Mexican government.

This only came in the passage of an Act, August 17, 1833, decreeing full secularization. The Act also provided for the colonization of both the Californias, the expenses of this latter move to be borne by the proceeds gained from the distribution of the Mission property. A shrewd politician named Hijars was to be made governor of Upper California for the purpose of carrying this law into effect.

But now Figueroa seemed to regret his first action. Perhaps it was jealousy that Hijars should have been appointed to his stead. He bitterly opposed Hijars, refused to give up the governorship, and after considerable " pulling and hauling," issued secularization orders of his own, greatly at variance with those promulgated by the Mexican Cortes, and proceeded to set them in operation.

Ten Missions were fully secularized in 1834, and six others in the following year. And now came the general scramble for Mission property. Each succeeding governor, freed from too close supervision by the general government in Mexico, which was passing through trials and tribulations of its own, helped himself to as much as he could get. Alvarado, from 1836 to 1842, plundered on every hand, and Pio Pico was not much better. When he became governor, there were few funds with which to carry on the affairs of the country, and he prevailed upon the assembly to pass a decree authorizing the renting or the sale of the Mission property, reserving only the church, a curate's house, and a building for a court-house. From the proceeds the expenses of conducting the services of the church were to be provided, but there was no disposition made as to what should be done to secure the funds for that purpose. Under this decree the final acts of spoliation were consummated.

The padres took the matter in accordance with their individual temperaments. Some were hopefully cheerful, and did the best they could for their Indian charges; others were sulky and sullen, and retired to the chambers allotted to them, coming forth only when necessary duty called; still others were belligerent, and fought everything and everybody, and, it must be confessed, generally with just cause.

As for the Indians, the effect was exactly as all thoughtful men had foreseen. Those who received property seldom made good use of it, and soon lost it. Cattle were neglected, tools unused, for there were none to compel their care or use. Consequently it was easy to convert them into money, which was soon gambled or drunk away. Rapidly they sank from worse to worse, until now only a few scattered settlements remain of the once vast number, thirty thousand or more, that were reasonably happy and prosperous under the rule of the padres.

CHAPTER IX

SAN DIEGO DE ALCALÁ

THE story of the founding of San Diego by Serra has already been given. It was the beginning of the realization of his fondest hopes. The early troubles with the Indians delayed conversions, but in 1773 Serra reported that some headway had been made. He gives the original name of the place as *Cosoy, in* 32° 43′, built on a hill two gunshots from the shore, and facing the entrance to the port at Point Guijarros. The missionaries left in charge were Padres Fernando Parron and Francisco Gomez.

About the middle of July ill health compelled Parron to retire to Lower California and Gomez to Mexico, and Padres Luis Jayme and Francisco Dumetz took their places.

San Diego was in danger of being abandoned for lack of provisions, for in 1772 Padre Crespí, who was at San Carlos, writes that on the thirtieth of March of that year "the mail reached us with the lamentable news that this Mission of San Diego was to be abandoned for lack of victuals." Serra then sent him with "twenty-two mules, and with them fifteen half-loads of flour" for their succor. Padres Dumetz and Cambon had gone out to hunt for food to the Lower California Missions. The same scarcity was noticed at San Gabriel, and the padres, " for a considerable time, already, had been using the supplies which were on hand to found the Mission of San Buenaventura; and though they have *drawn their belts tight* there remains to them provisions only for two months and a half."

Fortunately help came; so the work continued.

The region of San Diego was well peopled. At the time of the founding there were eleven rancherías within a radius of ten leagues. They must have been of a different type from most of the Indians of the coast, for, from the first, as the old Spanish chronicler reports, they were insolent, arrogant, and thievish. They lived on grass seeds, fish, and rabbits.

In 1774, the separation of the Mission from the presidio was decided upon, in order to remove the neophytes from the evil influences of the soldiers. The site chosen was six miles up the valley (named *Nipaguay* by the Indians), and so well did all work together that by the end of the year a dwelling, a storehouse, a smithy built of adobes, and a wooden church eighteen by fifty-seven feet, and roofed with tiles, were completed. Already the work of the padres had accomplished much. Seventy-six neophytes rejoiced their religious hearts, and the herds had increased to 40 cattle, 64 sheep, 55 goats, 19 hogs, 2 jacks, 2 burros, 17 mares, 3 foals, 9 horses, 22 mules, — 233 animals in all.

The presidio remained at Cosoy (now old San Diego), and four thousand adobes that had been made for the Mission buildings were turned over to the military. A rude stockade was erected, with two bronze cannon, one mounted towards the harbor, the other towards the Indian ranchería.

The experiments in grain raising at first were not successful. The seed was sown in the river bottom and the crop was destroyed by the unexpected rising of the river. The following year it was sown so far from water that it died from drought. In the fall of 1775 all seemed to be bright with hope. New buildings had been erected, a well dug, and more land made ready for sowing. The Indians were showing greater willingness to submit themselves to the priests, when a conflict occurred that revealed to the padres what they might have to contend with in their future efforts towards the Christianizing of the natives. The day before the feast of St. Francis (October 4, 1775), Padres Jayme and Fuster were made happy by being required to baptize sixty new converts. Yet a few days later they were saddened by the fact that two of these newly baptized fled from the Mission and escaped to the mountains, there to stir up enmity and revolt. For nearly a month they moved about, fanning the fires of hatred against the " long gowns," until on the night of November 4 (1775) nearly eight hundred naked savages, after dusk, stealthily advanced and surrounded the Mission, where the inmates slept unguarded, so certain were they of their security. Part of the force went on to the presidio, where, in the absence of the commander, the laxity of discipline was such that no sentinel was on guard.

An hour after midnight the whole of the Mission was surrounded. The quarters of the Christianized Indians were invaded, and they were threatened with instantaneous death if they gave the alarm. The church was broken into, and all the vestments and sacred vessels stolen. Then the buildings were fired. Not until then did the inmates know of their danger. Imagine their horror, to wake up and find the building on fire and themselves surrounded by what, in their dazed condition, seemed countless hordes of savages, all howling, yelling, brandishing war-clubs, firing their arrows, — the scene made doubly fearful by the red glare of the flames.

In the guard-house were four soldiers, — the whole of the Mission garrison; in the house the two priests, Jayme and Fuster, two little boys, and three men (a blacksmith and two carpenters). Father Fuster, the two boys, and the blacksmith sought to reach the guard-house, but the latter was slain on the way. The Indians broke into the room where the carpenters were, and one of them was so cruelly wounded that he died the next day.

Father Jayme, with the shining light of martyrdom in his eyes, and the fierce joy of fearlessness in his heart, not only refused to seek shelter, but deliberately walked towards the howling band, lifting his hands in blessing with his usual salutation: " Love God, my children! " Scarcely were the words uttered when the wild band fell upon him, shrieking and crying, tearing off his habit, thrusting him rudely along, hurting him with stones, sticks, and battle-axe, until at the edge of the creek his now naked body was bruised until life was extinct, and then the corpse filled with arrows.

Three soldiers and the carpenter, with Father Fuster and two boys loading the guns for them, fought off the invaders from a near-by kitchen, and at dawn the attacking force gathered up their dead and wounded and retired to the mountains.

No sooner were they gone than the neophytes came rushing up to see if any were left alive. Their delight at finding Father Fuster was immediately changed into sadness as others brought in the awfully mutilated and desecrated body of Father Jayme. Not until then did Father Fuster know that his companion was dead, and deep was the mourning of his inmost soul as he performed the last offices for his dear companion.

Strange to say, so careless was the garrison that not until a messenger reached it from Father Fuster did they know of the attack. They had placed no guards, posted no sentinels, and, indifferent in their foolish scorn of the prowess and courage of the Indians, had slept calmly, though they themselves might easily have been surprised, and the whole garrison murdered while asleep.

In the meantime letters were sent for aid to Rivera at Monterey, and Anza, the latter known to be approaching from the Colorado River region; and in suspense until they arrived, the little garrison and the remaining priests passed the rest of the year. The two commanders met at San Gabriel, and together marched to San Diego, where they arrived January 11, 1776. It was not long before they quarreled. Anza was for quick, decisive action; Rivera was for delay; so, when news arrived from San Gabriel that the food supply was running short, Anza left in order to carry out his original orders, which involved the founding of San Francisco. Not long after his departure Carlos, the neophyte who had been concerned in the insurrection, returned to San Diego, and, doubtless acting under the suggestion of the padres, took refuge in the temporary church at the presidio.

An unseemly squabble now ensued between Rivera and Padre Lasuen, the former violating the sanctuary of the church to arrest the Indian. Lasuen, on the next feast day, refused to say mass until Rivera and his violating officers had retired.

All this interfered with resumption of work on the church; so Serra himself went to San Diego, and, finding the ship " San Antonio " in the harbor, made an arrangement with Captain Choquet to supply sailors to do the building under his own direction. Rivera was then written to for a guard, and he sent six soldiers. On August 22, 1777, the three padres, Choquet with his mate and boatswain and twenty sailors, a company of neophytes, and the six soldiers went to the old site and began work in earnest, digging the foundations, making adobes, and collecting stones. The plan was to build a wall for defense, and then erect the church and other buildings inside. For fifteen days all went well. Then an Indian went to Rivera with a story that hostile Indians were preparing arrows for a new attack, and this so scared the gallant officer that he withdrew his six men. Choquet had to leave with his men, as he dared not take the responsibility of being away with so many men without the consent of Rivera; and, to the padre's great sorrow, the work had to cease.

In March of 1778 Captain Carrillo was sent to chastise hostile Indians at Pamó who had sent insolent messages to Captain Ortega. Carrillo surprised the foe, killed two, burned others who took refuge in a hut, while the others surrendered and were publicly flogged. The four chiefs, Aachel, Aalcuirin, Aaran, and Taguagui, were captured, taken to San Diego, and there shot, though the officer had no legal right to condemn even an Indian to death without the approval of the governor. Ortega's sentence reads: " Deeming it useful to the service of God, the King, and the public weal, I sentence them to a violent death by two musket-shots on the 11th at 9 A. M., the troops to be present at the execution under arms, also all the Christian rancherías subject to the San Diego Mission, that they may be warned to act righteously."

Ortega then instructed Padres Lasuen and Figuer to prepare the condemned. "You will co-operate for the good of their souls in the understanding that if they do not accept the salutary waters of baptism they die on Saturday morning; and if they do — they die all the same!" This was the first public execution in California.

In 1780 the new church, built of adobe, strengthened and roofed with pine timbers, ninety feet long and seventeen feet wide and high, was completed.

In 1782 fire destroyed the old presidio church.

In 1783 Lasuen made an interesting report on the condition of San Diego. At the Mission there were church, granary, storehouse, hospital, men's house, shed for wood and oven, two houses for the padres, larder, guest-room, and kitchen. These, with the soldiers' barracks, filled three sides of a square of about one hundred and sixty feet, and on the fourth side was an adobe wall, nearly ten feet high. There were seven hundred and forty neophytes at that time under missionary care, though Lasuen spoke most disparagingly of the location as a Mission site.

In 1824 San Diego registered its largest population, being then eighteen hundred and twenty-nine.

When Spanish rule ended, and the Mexican empire and republic sent its first governor, Echeandía, he decided to make San Diego his home; so for the period of his governorship, though he doubtless lived at or near the presidio, the Mission saw more or less of him. As is shown in the chapter on Secularization, he was engaged in a thankless task when he sought to change the Mission system, and there was no love lost between the governor's house and the Mission.

In 1833 Governor Figueroa visited San Diego Mission in person, in order to exhort the neophytes to seize the advantages of citizenship which the new secularization regulations were to give to them; but, though they heard him patiently, and there and at San Luis Rey one hundred and sixty families were found to be duly qualified for "freedom," only ten could be found to accept it.

On March 29, 1843, Governor Micheltorena issued a decree which restored San Diego Mission temporalities to the management of the padre. He explained in his prelude that the decree was owing to the fact that the Mission establishments had been reduced to the mere space occupied by the buildings and orchards, that the padres had no support but that of charity, etc. Mofras gives the number of Indians in 1842 as five hundred, but an official report of 1844 gives only one hundred.   The Mission retained the ranches of Santa Isabel and El Cajon until 1844–1845, and then, doubtless, they were sold or rented in accordance with the plans of Pio Pico.

To-day nothing but the *fachada* of the church remains, and that has recently been braced or it would have fallen.   There are a few portions of walls also, and a large part of the adobe wall around the garden remains.   The present owner of the orchard, in digging up some of the old olive trees, has found a number of interesting relics, stirrups, a gun-barrel, hollow iron cannon-balls, metates, etc.   These are all preserved and shown as " curios," together with beams from the church, and the old olive-mill.

By the side of the ruined church a newer and modern brick building now stands.   It destroys the picturesqueness of the old site, but it is engaged in a good work.   Father Ubach, the indefatigable parish priest of San Diego, who died a few years ago, and who was possessed of the spirit of the old padres, erected this building for the training of the Indian children of the region.   On one occasion I asked the children if they knew any of the " songs of the old," the songs their Indian grandparents used to sing; and to my delight, they sang two of the old chorals taught their ancestors in the early Mission days by the padres.

Photograph by Fred W. Twogood, Riverside.

FACHADA OF THE RUINED MISSION OF SAN DIEGO.

OLD MISSION OF SAN DIEGO
AND SISTERS' SCHOOL FOR INDIAN CHILDREN.

THE TOWER AT MISSION SAN CARLOS BORROMEO, CARMEL VALLEY, MONTEREY.

MAIN ENTRANCE ARCH AT MISSION SAN DIEGO.

CHAPTER X

A BRIEF account of the founding of San Carlos
at Monterey, June 3, 1770, was given in an earlier
chapter. What joy the discovery of the harbor
and founding of the Mission caused in Mexico
and Spain can be understood when it is remembered that for two centuries this thing had been
desired. In the Mexican city the bells of the
Cathedral rang forth merry peals as on special
festival days, and a solemn mass of thanksgiving
was held, at which all the city officials and dignitaries were present. A full account of the event
was printed and distributed there and in Spain, so
that, for a time at least, California occupied a
large share of public attention.

The result of the news of the founding of San
Carlos was that all were enthused for further
extension of the Missions. The indefatigable
Galvez at once determined that five new Missions
should be founded, and the Guardian of the Franciscan College was asked for, and agreed to send,
ten more missionaries for the new establishments,
as well as twenty for the old and new Missions
on the peninsula.

At the end of the year 1773 Serra made his report to Mexico, and then it was found that there were more converts at San Carlos than at any other Mission. Three Spanish soldiers had married native women.

A little later, as the mud roofs were not successful in keeping out the winter rains, a new church was built, partly of rough and partly of worked lumber, and roofed with tules. The lumber used was the pine and cypress for which the region is still noted.

There was little agriculture, only five fanegas of wheat being harvested in 1772. Each Mission received eighteen head of horned cattle at its founding, and San Carlos reported a healthy increase.

In 1772 Serra left for Mexico, to lay matters from the missionary standpoint before the new viceroy, Bucareli. He arrived in the city of Mexico in February, 1773. With resistless energy and eloquence he pleaded for the preservation of the shipyard of San Blas, the removal of Fages, the correction of certain abuses that had arisen as the result of Fages's actions, and for further funds, soldiers, etc., to prosecute the work of founding more Missions. In all the main points his mission was successful. Captain Rivera y Moncada, with whose march from the peninsula we are already familiar, was appointed governor; and at the same time that he received his instructions, August 17, 1773, Captain Juan Bautista de Anza was authorized to attempt the overland journey from Sonora to Monterey.

As we have already seen, this trip was successful and led to the second, in which the colonists and soldiers for the new Mission of San Francisco were brought.

In 1776 Serra's heart was joyed with the thought that he was to wear a martyr's crown, for there was a rumor of an Indian uprising at San Carlos; but the presence of troops sent over from Monterey seemed to end the trouble.

In 1779 a maritime event of importance occurred. The padres at San Carlos and the soldiers at Monterey saw a galleon come into the bay, which proved to be the "San José," from Manila. It should have remained awhile, but contrary winds arose, and it sailed away for San Lucas. But the king later issued orders that all Manila galleons must call at Monterey, under a penalty of four thousand dollars, unless prevented by stress of weather.

In 1784 Serra died and was buried at San Carlos.

For a short time after Serra's death, the duties of padre presidente fell upon Palou; but in February, 1785, the college of San Fernando elected Lasuen to the office, and thereafter he resided mainly at San Carlos.

September 14, 1786, the eminent French navigator, Jean François Galaup de la Pérouse, with two vessels, appeared at Monterey, and the Frenchman in the account of his trip gives us a vivid

picture of his reception at the Mission of San
Carlos.

A few years later Vancouver, the English
navigator, also visited San Francisco, Santa
Clara, and San Carlos. He was hospitably entertained by Lasuen, but when he came again, he
was not received so warmly, doubtless owing to
the fearfulness of the Spaniards as to England's
intentions.

When Pico issued his decrees in 1845, San Carlos
was regarded as a pueblo, or abandoned Mission,
Padre Real residing at Monterey and holding services only occasionally. The little property that
remained was to be sold at auction for the payment
of debts and the support of worship, but there
is no record of property, debts, or sale. The glory
of San Carlos was departed.

For many years no one cared for the building,
and it was left entirely to the mercy of the vandal
and relic hunter. In 1852 the tile roof fell in,
and all the tiles, save about a thousand, were either
then broken, or afterwards stolen. The rains and
storms beating in soon brought enough sand to
form a lodgment for seeds, and ere long a dense
growth of grass and weeds covered the dust of
California's great apostle.

In *Glimpses of California* by H. H., Mr. Sand-
ham, the artist, has a picture which well illus-
trates the original spring of the roof and curve
of the walls. There were three buttresses, *from
which* sprang the roof arches. The curves of the

walls were made by increasing the thickness at the top, as can be seen from the window spaces on each side, which still remain in their original condition. The building is about one hundred and fifty feet long by thirty feet wide.

In 1868 Rev. Angelo D. Cassanova became the pastor of the parish church at Monterey, and though Serra's home Mission was then a complete mass of ruins, he determined upon its preservation, at least from further demolition. The first step was to clear away the débris that had accumulated since its abandonment, and then to locate the graves of the missionaries. On July 3, 1882, after due notice in the San Francisco papers, over four hundred people assembled at San Carlos, the stone slab was removed, and the bodies duly identified.

The discovery of the bodies of Serra, Crespí, Lopez, and Lasuen aroused some sentiment and interest in Father Cassanova's plan of restoration; and sufficient aid came to enable him properly to restore and roof the building. On August 28, 1884, the rededication took place, and the building was left as it is found to-day.

The old pulpit still remains. It is reached by steps from the sacristy through a doorway in the main side wall. It is a small and unpretentious structure of wood, with wooden sounding-board above. It rests upon a solid stone pedestal, cut into appropriate shaft and mouldings. The door is of solid oak, substantially built.

In the sacristy is a double lavatory of solid

sandstone, hewn and arranged for flowing water. It consists of two basins, one above the other, the latter one well recessed. The lower basin is structurally curved in front, and the whole piece is of good and artistic workmanship.

In the neighborhood of San Carlos there are enough residents to make up a small congregation, and it is the desire of Father Mestris, the present priest at Monterey, to establish a parish there, have a resident minister, and thus restore the old Mission to its original purpose.

CHAPTER XI

BEFORE leaving San Carlos it will be well to explain the facts in regard to the Mission church at Monterey. Many errors have been perpetuated about this church. There is little doubt but that originally the Mission was established here, and the first church built on this site. But as I have elsewhere related, Padre Serra found it unwise to have the Indians and the soldiers too near together.

In the establishment of the Missions, the presidios were founded to be a means of protection to the padres in their work of civilizing and Christianizing the natives. These presidios were at San Diego, Monterey, San Francisco, and Santa Barbara. Each was supposed to have its own church or chapel, and the original intention was that each should likewise have its own resident priest. For purposes of economy, however, this was not done, and the Mission padres were called upon for this service, though it was often a source of disagreement between the military and the missionaries. While the Monterey church that occupied the site of the present structure may, in the first instance, have been used by Serra for the Mission, it was later used as the church for the soldiers, and thus became the presidio chapel. I have been unable to learn when it was built, but about fifty years ago Governor Pacheco donated the funds for its enlargement. The original building was extended back a number of feet, and an addition made, which makes the church of cruciform shape, the original building being the long arm of the cross. The walls are built of sandstone rudely quarried at the rear of the church. It is now the parish church of Monterey.

Here are a large number of interesting relics and memorials of Serra and the early Mission days. The chief of these is a reliquary case, made by an Indian at San Carlos to hold certain valuable relics which Serra highly prized. Some of these are bones from the Catacombs, and an Agnus Dei of wax. Serra himself wrote the list of contents on a slip of paper, which is still intact on the back of the case. This reliquary used to be carried in procession by Serra on each fourth of November, and is now used by Father Mestris in like ceremonials.

In the altar space or sanctuary are five chairs, undoubtedly brought to California by one of the Philippine galleons from one of those islands, or from China. The bodies are of teak, ebony, or ironwood, with seats of marble, and with a disk of marble in the back.

PRESIDIO CHURCH AND PRIESTS RESIDENCE, MONTEREY, CALIF.

Copyright, 1904, by C.C. Pierce & Co.

MISSION SAN CARLOS.

Photograph by George Wharton James.

MISSION SAN ANTONIO DE PADUA

PRESIDIO CHURCH, MONTEREY

In the sacristy is the safe in which Serra used to keep the sacred vessels, as well as the important papers connected with his office. It is an interesting object, sheeted with iron, wrapped around with iron bands and covered all over with bosses. It is about three feet wide and four feet high. In the drawers close by are several of the copes, stoles, maniples, and other vestments which were once used by Serra at the old Mission.

CHAPTER XII

SAN ANTONIO DE PADUA

THE third Mission of the series was founded in honor of San Antonio de Padua, July 14, 1771, by Serra, accompanied by Padres Pieras and Sitjar. One solitary Indian heard the dedicatory mass, but Serra's enthusiasm knew no bounds. He was assured that this " first fruit of the wilderness " would go forth and bring many of his companions to the priests. Immediately after the mass he hastened to the Indian, lavished much attention on him, and gave him gifts. That same day many other Indians came and clearly indicated a desire to stay with such pleasant company. They brought pine-nuts and acorns, and the padres gave them in exchange strings of glass beads of various colors.

At once buildings were begun, in which work the Indians engaged with energy, and soon church and dwellings, surrounded by a palisade, were completed. From the first the Indians manifested confidence in the padres, and the fifteen days that Padre Serra remained were days of intense joy and gladness at seeing the readiness of the natives to associate with him and his brother priests. Without delay they began to learn the language of the Indians, and when they had made sufficient progress they devoted much time to catechising them. In two years 158 natives were baptized and enrolled, and instead of relying upon the missionaries for food, they brought in large quantities of acorns, pine-nuts, squirrels, and rabbits. The Mission being located in the heart of the mountains, where pine and oak trees grew luxuriantly, the pine-nut and acorn were abundant. Before the end of 1773 the church and dwellings were all built, of adobe, and three soldiers, who had married native women, were living in separate houses.

In August of 1774 occurred the first trouble. The gentile Indians, angered at the progress of the Mission and the gathering in of so many of their people, attacked the Mission and wounded an Indian about to be baptized. When the news reached Rivera at Monterey, he sent a squad of soldiers, who captured the culprits, gave them a flogging, and imprisoned them. Later they were flogged again, and, after a few days in the stocks, they were released.

In 1779 an alcalde and regidore were chosen from the natives to assist in the administration of justice. In 1800 the report shows that the neophyte population was 1118, with 767 baptisms and 656 deaths. The cattle and horses had decreased from 2232 of the last report to 2217, but small stock had slightly increased. In 1787 the church was regarded as the best in California, though it was much improved later, for in 1797 it is stated that it was of adobes with a tiled roof. In 1793 the large adobe block, eighty varas long and one vara wide, was constructed for friars' houses, church and storehouse, and it was doubtless this church that was tiled four years later.

In 1805 it gained its highest population, there being 1296 Indians under its control. The lands of the Mission were found to be barren, necessitating frequent changes in cultivated fields and stock ranges.

In 1808 the venerable Buenaventura Sitjar, one of the founders of the Mission, and who had toiled there continuously for thirty-seven years, passed to his reward, and was buried in sight of the hills he had loved so long. The following year, or in 1810, work was begun on a newer and larger church of adobes, and this is doubtless the building whose ruins now remain. Though we have no record of its dedication, there is no question but that it took place prior to 1820, and in 1830 references are made to its arched corridors, etc., built of brick. Robinson, who visited it in this year, says the whole Mission is built of brick, but in this he is in error. The *fachada* is of brick, but the main part of the building is of adobe. Robinson speaks thus of the Mission and its friar: "Padre Pedro Cabot, the present missionary director, I found to be a fine, noble-looking man, whose manner and whole deportment would have

Photograph by Harold A Parker, Pasadena.

RUINS OF MISSION SAN ANTONIO DE PADUA.

Photograph by C.C. Pierce & Co., Los Angeles.

DUTTON HOTEL, JOLON.

On the old stage route between San Francisco and Los Angeles,
near Mission San Antonio de Padua.

RUINED CORRIDORS AT SAN ANTONIO DE PADUA.

led one to suppose he had been bred in the courts of Europe, rather than in the cloister. Everything was in the most perfect order: the Indians cleanly and well dressed, the apartments tidy, the workshops, granaries, and storehouses comfortable and in good keeping."

In 1834 Cabot retired to give place to Padre Jesus María Vasquez del Mercado, one of the newly arrived Franciscans from Zacatecas. In this year the neophyte population had dwindled to 567, and five years later Visitador Hartwell found only 270 living at the Mission and its adjoining ranches. It is possible, however, that there were fully as many more living at a distance of whom he gained no knowledge, as the official report for 1840 gives 500 neophytes.

Manuel Crespo was the comisionado for secularization in 1835, and he and Padre Mercado had no happy times together. Mercado made it so unpleasant that six other administrators were appointed in order to please him, but it was a vain attempt. As a consequence, the Indians felt the disturbances and discord, and became discontented and unmanageable.

In 1843, according to Governor Micheltorena's order of March 29, the temporal control of the Mission was restored to the padre. But, though the order was a kindly one, and relieved the padre from the interference of officious, meddling, inefficient, and dishonest " administrators," it was too late to effect any real service.

As far as I can learn, Pico's plan did not affect San Antonio, and it was not one of those sold by him in 1845–1846. In 1848 Padre Doroteo Ambris was in charge as curate. For thirty years he remained here, true to his calling, an entirely different kind of man from the quarrelsome, arrogant, drinking, and gambling Mercado. He finally died at San Antonio, and was buried in the Mission he guarded so well.

In 1904 the California Historic Landmarks League (Inc.) undertook the preservation of San Antonio, but little has yet been accomplished. Much more should speedily be done, if the walls are to be kept from falling.

CHAPTER XIII

SAN GABRIEL, ARCÁNGEL

WE have already seen that San Gabriel, the fourth Mission, was founded September 8, 1771. The natives gave cheerful assistance in bringing timber, erecting the wooden buildings, covering them with tules, and constructing the stockade enclosure which surrounded them. They also brought offerings of acorns and pine-nuts. In a few days so many of them crowded into camp that Padre Somero went to San Diego for an addition to the guard, and returned with two extra men. It was not long before the soldiers got into trouble, owing to their treatment of the Indian women, and an Indian attack, as before related, took place. A few days later, Fages appeared on the scene from San Diego with sixteen soldiers and two missionaries, who were destined as guard and priests for the new Mission of San Buenaventura. But the difficulty with the Indians led Fages to postpone the founding of the new Mission. The offending soldier was hurried off to Monterey to get him out of the way of further trouble. The padres did their best to correct the evil impression the soldiers had created, and, strange to say, the first child brought for baptism was the son of the chief who had been killed in the dispute with the soldiers.

But the San Gabriel soldiers were not to be controlled. They were insolent to the aged priests, who were in ill-health; they abused the Indians so far as to pursue them to their rancherías " for the fun of the thing ; " and there they had additional " sport " by lassoing the women and killing such men as interfered with their lusts. No wonder Serra's heart was heavy when he heard the news, and that he attributed the small number of baptisms — only seventy-three in two years — to the wickedness of the men who should have aided instead of hindering the work.

In his first report to Mexico, Serra tells of the Indian population around San Gabriel. He says it is larger than at any other Mission, though, unfortunately, of several different tribes who are at war with one another; and the tribes nearest to the sea will not allow others to fish, so that they are often in great want of food. Of the prospects for agriculture he is most enthusiastic. The location is a well-watered plain, with plenty of water and natural facilities for irrigation; and though the first year's crop was drowned out, the second produced one hundred and thirty fanegas of maize and seven fanegas of beans. The buildings erected are of the same general character as those already described at San Carlos, though somewhat smaller.

When Captain Anza reached California from

INTERIOR OF MISSION, SAN ANTONIO DE PADUA

REAR OF CHURCH, MISSION SAN ANTONIO DE PADUA.

RUINS OF THE ARCHES, MISSION SAN ANTONIO DE PADUA.

MISSION SAN GABRIEL ARCANGEL.

Sonora, by way of the Colorado, on his first trip
in 1774, accompanied by Padre Garcés, he stayed
for awhile to recuperate at San Gabriel; and
when he came the second time, with the colonists
for the new presidio of San Francisco, San Gabriel
was their first real stopping-place after that long,
weary, and arduous journey across the sandy
deserts of Arizona and California. Here Anza
met Rivera, who had arrived the day before from
Monterey. It will be remembered that just at
that time the news came of the Indian uprising
at San Diego; so, leaving his main force and the
immigrants to recuperate, he and seventeen of
his soldiers, with Padre Font, started with Rivera
for the south. This was in January, 1776. He
and Rivera did not agree as to the best methods
to be followed in dealing with the troublesome
Indians; so, when advices reached him from San
Gabriel that provisions were giving out, he decided
to allow Rivera to follow his own plans, but that
he would wait no longer. When he arrived at San
Gabriel, February 12, he found that three of his
muleteers, a servant, and a soldier belonging to
the Mission had deserted, taking with them
twenty-five horses and a quantity of Mission
property. His ensign, Moraga, was sent after
the deserters; but, as he did not return as soon
as was expected, Anza started with his band of
colonists for the future San Francisco, where
they duly arrived, as is recorded in the San Francisco chapter.

In 1777-1778 the Indians were exceedingly troublesome, and on one occasion came in large force, armed, to avenge some outrage the soldiers had perpetrated. The padres met them with a shining image of Our Lady, when, immediately, they were subdued, and knelt weeping at the feet of the priests.

In October, 1785, trouble was caused by a woman tempting (so they said) the neophytes and gentiles to attack the Mission and kill the padres. The plot was discovered, and the corporal in command captured some twenty of the leaders and quelled the uprising without bloodshed. Four of the ringleaders were imprisoned, the others whipped with fifteen or twenty lashes each, and released. The woman was sentenced to perpetual exile, and possibly shipped off to one of the peninsula Missions.

In 1810 the settlers at Los Angeles complained to the governor that the San Gabriel padres had dammed up the river at Cahuenga, thus cutting off their water supply; and they also stated that the padres refused to attend to the spiritual wants of their sick. The padres offered to remove the dam if the settlers were injured thereby, and also claimed that they were always glad to attend to the sick when their own pressing duties allowed.

On January 14, 1811, Padre Francisco Dumetz, one of Serra's original compadres, died at San Gabriel. At this time, and since 1806, Padre

José María Zalvidea, that strict martinet of padres, was in charge, and he brought the Mission up to its highest state of efficiency. He it was who began the erection of the stone church that now remains, and the whole precinct, during his rule, rang with the busy hammer, clatter, chatter, and movement of a large number of active workers.

It was doubtless owing to the earthquake of December 8, 1812, which occurred at sunrise, that a new church was built. The main altar was overthrown, several of the figures broken, the steeple toppled over and crashed to the ground, and the sacristy walls were badly cracked. The padres' house as well as all the other buildings suffered.

One of the adjuncts to San Gabriel was *El Molino Viejo*, — the old mill. Indeed there were *two* old mills, the first one, however, built in Padre Zalvidea's time, in 1810 to 1812, being the one that now remains. It is about two miles from the Mission. It had to be abandoned on account of faulty location. Being built on the hillside, its west main wall was the wall of the deep funnel-shaped cisterns which furnished the water head. This made the interior damp. Then, too, the chamber in which the water-well revolved was so low that the powerful head of water striking the horizontal wheel splashed all over the walls and worked up through the shaft holes to the mill stones and thus wet the flour. This necessitated the constant presence of Indian women to carry away the meal to dry storerooms at the Mission, where it was bolted by a hand process of their own devising. On this account the mill was abandoned, and for several years the whole of the meal for the Mission was ground on the old-style metates.

The region adjacent to the mill was once largely inhabited by Indians, for the foreman of the mill ranch declares that he has hauled from the adjacent bluff as many stone pestles and mortars, metates and grinders as would load a four-horse wagon.

It should not be forgotten that originally the mill was roofed with red tiles made by the Indians at the Mission; but these have entirely disappeared.

It was the habit of Padre Zalvidea to send certain of his most trusted neophytes over to the islands of San Clemente and Catalina with a "bolt" or two of woven serge, made at the Mission San Gabriel, to exchange with the island Indians for their soapstone cooking vessels, — mortars, etc. These traders embarked from a point where Redondo now is, and started always at midnight.

In 1819 the Indians of the Guachama rancho, called San Bernardino, petitioned for the introduction of agriculture and stock raising, and this was practically the beginning of that *asistencia*, as will be recorded in the chapter on the various chapels. A chapel was also much needed at Puente, where Zalvidea had six hundred Indians at work in 1816.

In 1822 San Gabriel was fearfully alarmed at the rumor that one hundred and fifty Indians were bearing down upon that Mission from the Colorado River region. It transpired that it was an Opata with despatches, and that the company had no hostile intent. But Captain Portilla met them and sent them back, not a little disconcerted by their inhospitable reception.

Of the wild, political chaos that occurred in California after Mexico became independent of Spain, San Gabriel felt occasional waves. When the people of San Diego and the southern part of the State rebelled against Governor Victoria, and the latter confident chief came to arrange matters, a battle took place near Los Angeles, in which he was severely wounded. His friends bore him to San Gabriel, and, though he had entirely defeated his foes, so cleverly did some one work upon his fears that he made a formal surrender, December 6, 1831. On the ninth the leader of the rebels, the former Governor Echeandía, had a conference with him at San Gabriel, where he pledged himself to return to Mexico without giving further trouble; and on the twentieth he left, stopping for awhile at San Luis Rey with Padre Peyri. It was at this time the venerable and worthy Peyri decided to leave California, and he therefore accompanied the deposed governor to San Diego, from which port they sailed January 17, 1832.

After secularization San Gabriel was one of the Missions that slaughtered a large number of her cattle for the hides and tallow. Pio Pico states that he had the contract at San Gabriel, employing ten vaqueros and thirty Indians, and that he thus killed over five thousand head. Robinson says that the rascally contractors secretly appropriated two hides for every one they turned over to the Mission.

In 1843, March 29, Micheltorena's order, restoring San Gabriel to the padres, was carried out, and in 1844 the official church report states that nothing is left but its vineyards in a sad condition, and three hundred neophytes. The final inventory made by the comisionados under Pio Pico is missing, so that we do not know at what the Mission was valued; but June 8, 1846, he sold the whole property to Reid and Workman in payment for past services to the government. When attacked for his participation in what evidently seemed the fraudulent transfer of the Mission, Pico replies that the sale " did not go through." The United States officers, in August of the same year, dispossessed the " purchasers," and the courts finally decreed the sale invalid.

There are a few portions of the old cactus hedge still remaining, planted by Padre Zalvidea. Several hundreds of acres of vineyard and garden were thus enclosed for purposes of protection from Indians and roaming bands of horses and cattle. The fruit of the prickly pear was a prized article of diet by the Indians, so that the hedge was of benefit in two ways, — protection and food.

On the altar are several of the old statues, and there are some quaint pictures upon the walls.

In the baptistry is a font of hammered copper, probably made either at San Gabriel or San Fernando. There are several other interesting vessels. At the rear of the church are the remains of five brick structures, where the soap-making and tallow-rendering of the Mission was conducted. Five others were removed a few years ago to make way for the public road. Undoubtedly there were other buildings for the women and male neophytes as well as the workshops.

The San Gabriel belfry is well known in picture, song, and story. Yet the fanciful legends about the casting of the bells give way to stern fact when they are examined. Upon the first bell is the inscription: "Ave María Santisima. S. Francisco. De Paula Rvelas, me fecit." The second: "Cast by G. H. Holbrook, Medway, Mass., 1828." The third: "Ave Maria, Sn Jvan Nepomvseno, Rvelas me fecit, A. D., '95." The fourth: "Fecit Benitvs a Regibvs, Ano D. 1830, Sn. Frano."

In the year 1886 a number of needed repairs were made; the windows were enlarged, and a new ceiling put in, the latter a most incongruous piece of work.

CHAPTER XIV

SAN LUIS OBISPO DE TOLOSA

FOUNDED, as we have seen, by Serra himself, September 1, 1772, by the end of 1773 the Mission of San Luis Obispo could report only twelve converts. Serra left the day after the founding, leaving Padre Cavaller in charge, with two Indians from Lower California, four soldiers and their corporal. Their only provisions were a few hundred pounds of flour and wheat, and a barrel of brown sugar. But the Indians were kind, in remembrance of Fages's goodness in shooting the bears, and brought them venison and seeds frequently, so they " managed to subsist " until provisions came.

Padre Cavaller built a neat chapel of logs and apartments for the missionaries, and the soldiers soon erected their own barracks. While the Indians were friendly, they did not seem to be particularly attracted to the Mission, as they had more and better food than the padre, and the only thing he had that they particularly desired was cloth. There was no ranchería in the vicinity, but they were much interested in the growth of the corn and beans sown by the padre, and which,

MISSION SAN GABRIEL ARCANGEL.

SAN LUIS OBISPO, BEFORE RESTORATION.

Photograph by Harold A. Parker, Pasadena.

RUINED MISSION OF SAN JUAN CAPISTRANO.

Showing campanile and protected arched corridors. See page 136.

Photograph by C.C. Pierce & Co., Los Angeles.

THE RESTORED MISSION OF SAN LUIS OBISPO.

being on good and well-watered land, yielded
abundantly.

In 1776 certain gentiles, who were hostile to
some Indians that were sheltered by the padres,
attacked the Mission by discharging burning
arrows upon the tule roof of the buildings, and
everything was destroyed, save the church and
the granary. Rivera came at once, captured two
of the ringleaders, and sent them for punishment to the Monterey presidio. The success of
the gentiles led them to repeat their attacks
by setting fire to the Mission twice during the
next ten years, and it was these calamities that
led one of the San Luis padres to attempt the
making of roof tiles. Being successful, it was not
long before all the Missions were so roofed.

In 1794 certain of the neophytes of San Luis
and La Purísima conspired with some gentiles
to incite the Indians at San Luis to revolt, but
the arrest and deportation of fifteen or twenty
of the ringleaders to Monterey, to hard labor at
the presidio, put a stop to the revolt.

Padres Lasuen and Tapis both served here as
missionaries, and in 1798 Luis Antonio Martinez,
one of the best known of the padres, began his
long term of service at San Luis. In 1794 the
Mission reached its highest population of 946
souls. It had 6500 head of cattle and horses,
6150 sheep. In 1798 it raised 4100 bushels of
wheat, and in this same year a water-power mill
was erected and set in motion. San Luis was

also favored by the presence of a smith, a miller, and a carpenter of the artisan instructors, sent by the king in 1794. Looms were erected, and cotton brought up from San Blas was woven. A new church of adobes, with a tile roof, was completed in 1793, and that same year a portico was added to its front.

In 1830 Padre Martinez was banished to Madrid, and at this time the buildings at San Luis were already falling into decay, as the padre, with far-seeing eye, was assured that the politicians had nothing but evil in store for them. Consequently, he did not keep up things as he otherwise would have done. He was an outspoken, frank, fearless man, and this undoubtedly led to his being chosen as the example necessary to restrain the other padres from too great freedom of speech and manner.

In 1834 San Luis had 264 neophytes, though after secularization the number was gradually reduced until, in 1840, there were but 170 left. The order of secularization was put into effect in 1835 by Manuel Jimeno Casarin. The inventory of the property in 1836 showed $70,000. In 1839 it was $60,000. In 1840 all the horses were stolen by " New Mexican traders," one report alone telling of the driving away of 1200 head. The officers at Los Angeles went in pursuit of the thieves and one party reported that it came in full sight of the foe retiring deliberately with the stolen animals, but, as there were as many

Americans as Indians in the band, they deemed it imprudent to risk a conflict.

In December of 1846, when Frémont was marching south to co-operate with Stockton against the Southern Californians, San Luis was thought to harbor an armed force of hostiles. Accordingly Frémont surrounded it one dark, rainy night, and took it by sudden assault. The fears were unfounded, for only women, children, and noncombatants were found.

The Book of Confirmations at San Luis has its introductory pages written by Serra. There is also a " Nota " opposite page three, and a full-page note in the back in his clear, vigorous and distinctive hand.

There are three bells at San Luis Obispo. The largest is to the right, the smallest in the center. On the largest bell is the following inscription: " Me fecit ano di 1818 Manvel Vargas, Lima. Mision de Sn Luis Obispo De La Nueba California." This latter is a circumferential panel about midway between the top and bottom of the bell. On the middle bell we read the same inscription, while there is none on the third. This latter was cast in San Francisco, from two old bells which were broken.

From a painting the old San Luis Obispo church is seen to have been raised up on a stone and cement foundation. The corridor was without the arches that are elsewhere one of the distinctive features, but plain round columns, with a square base and topped with a plain square moulding, gave support to the roof beams, on which the usual red-tiled roof was placed.

The *fachada* of the church retreats some fifteen or twenty feet from the front line of the corridors. The monastery has been " restored," even as has the church, out of all resemblance to its own honest original self. The adobe walls are covered with painted wood, and the tiles have given way to shingles, just like any other modern and commonplace house. The building faces the southeast. The altar end is at the northwest. To the southwest are the remains of a building of boulders, brick, and cement, exactly of the same style as the asistencia building of Santa Margarita. It seems as if it might have been built by the same hands. Possibly in the earlier days Santa Margarita was a *vista* of San Luis, rather than of San Miguel, though it is generally believed that it was under the jurisdiction of the latter.

CHAPTER XV

THE story of Bucareli's determination to found a presidio at San Francisco, and Anza's march with the colonists for it from Sonora, has already been recounted. When Serra and Galvez were making their original plans for the establishment of the three first Missions of Alta California, Serra expressed his disappointment that St. Francis was neglected by asking: " And for our founder St. Francis there is no Mission? " To which Galvez replied: " If St. Francis desires a Mission, let him show us his harbor and he shall have one." It therefore seemed providential that when Portolá, Fages, and Crespí, in 1769, saw the Bay of Monterey they did not recognize it, and were thus led on further north, where the great Bay of San Francisco was soon afterwards discovered and reasonably well surveyed.

Palou eventually established the Mission October 9, 1776. None of the Indians were present to witness the ceremony, as they had fled, the preceding month, from the attacks of certain of their enemies. When they returned in December they brought trouble with them. They stole all in their reach; one party discharged arrows at the corporal of the guard; another insulted a soldier's wife; and an attempt was made to kill the San Carlos neophyte who had been 'brought here. The officers shut up one of these hostiles, whereat a party of his comrades rushed to the rescue, fired their arrows at the Mission, and were only driven back when the soldiers arrived and fired their muskets in the air. Next day the sergeant went out to make arrests and another struggle ensued, in which one was killed and one wounded. All now sued for peace, which, with sundry floggings, was granted. For three months they now kept away from the Mission.

In 1777 they began to return, and on October 4, Padre Serra, on his first visit, was able to say mass in the presence of seventeen adult native converts. Then, passing over to the presidio on October 10, as he stood gazing on the waters flowing out to the setting sun through the purple walls of the Golden Gate, he exclaimed with a heart too full of thanksgiving to be longer restrained: " Thanks be to God that now our father St. Francis with the Holy Cross of the Procession of Missions, has reached the last limit of the Californian continent. To go farther he must have boats."

In 1782, April 25, the corner-stone of a new church was laid at San Francisco. Three padres were present, together with the Mission guard and a body of troops from the presidio. In the Mission records it says: "There was enclosed in the cavity of said corner-stone the image of our Holy Father St. Francis, some relics in the form of bones of St. Pius and other holy martyrs, five medals of various saints, and a goodly portion of silver coin."

In 1785 Governor Fages complained to the viceroy, among other things, that the presidio of San Francisco had been deprived of mass for three years, notwithstanding the obligation of the friars to serve as chaplains. Palou replied that the padres were under no obligation to serve gratuitously, and that they were always ready to attend the soldiers when their other duties allowed.

In November, 1787, Captain Soler, who for a brief time acted as temporary governor and inspector, suggested that the presidio of San Francisco be abandoned and its company trans-ferred to Santa Barbara. Later, as I have shown elsewhere, a proposition was again made for the abandonment of San Francisco; so it is apparent that Fate herself was protecting it for its future great and wonderful history.

In 1790 San Francisco reported 551 baptisms and 205 deaths, with a present neophyte popula-tion of 438. Large stock had increased to 2000 head and small to 1700.

Three years later, on November 14, the cele-brated English navigator, George Vancouver, in his vessel "Discovery," sailed into San Francisco

Bay. His arrival caused quite a flutter of excitement both at the presidio and Mission, where he was kindly entertained. The governor was afraid of this elaborate hospitality to the hated and feared English, and issued orders to the commandant providing for a more frigid reception in the future, so, on Vancouver's second visit, he did not find matters so agreeable, and grumbled accordingly.

Tiles were made and put on the church roofs in 1795; more houses were built for the neophytes, and all roofed with tiles. Half a league of ditch was also dug around the potrero (pasture ground) and fields.

In 1806 San Francisco was enlivened by the presence of the Russian chamberlain, Rezánof, who had been on a special voyage around the world, and was driven by scurvy and want of provisions to the California settlements. He was accompanied by Dr. G. H. von Langsdorff. Langsdorff's account of the visit and reception at several points in California is interesting. He gives a full description of the Indians and their method of life at the Mission; commends the zeal and self-sacrifice of the padres; speaks of the ingenuity shown by the women in making baskets; the system of allowing the cattle and horses to run wild, etc. Visiting the Mission of San José by boat, he and his companions had quite an adventurous time getting back, owing to the contrary winds.

Rezánof's visit and its consequences have been made the subject of much and romantic writing. Gertrude Atherton's novel, *Rezánof*, is devoted to this episode in his life. The burden of the story is possibly true, viz., that the Russians in their settlements to the north were suffering for want of the food that California was producing in abundance. Yet, owing to the absurd Spanish laws governing California, she was forbidden to sell to or trade with any foreign peoples or powers. Rezánof, who was well acquainted with this prohibitory law, determined upon trying to overcome it for the immediate relief of his suffering compatriots. He was fairly well received when he reached San Francisco, but he could accomplish nothing in the way of trading or the sale of the needed provisions.

Now began a campaign of strategic waiting. To complicate (or simplify) the situation, in the *bailes* and *festas* given to the distinguished Russian, Rezánof danced and chatted with Concha Argüello, the daughter of the stern old commandant of the post.

Did they fall in love with each other, or did they not? Some writers say one thing and some another. Anyhow, the girl thought she had received the honest love of a noble man and responded with ardor and devotion. So sure was she of his affection that she finally prevailed upon her father (so we are told) to sell to Rezánof the provisions for which he had come. The vessel, accordingly, was well and satisfactorily laden, and Rezánof sailed away. Being a Russian subject, he was not allowed to marry the daughter of a foreigner without the consent of his sovereign, and he was to hurry to Moscow and gain permission to return and wed the lady of his choice.

He never returned. Hence the accusation that he acted in bad faith to her and her father. This charge seems to be unfounded, for it is known that he left his vessel and started overland to reach Moscow earlier than he could have done by ship, that he was taken seriously ill on the trip and died.

But Concha did not know of this. No one informed her of the death of her lover, and her weary waiting for his return is what has given the touch of keenest pathos to the romantic story. Bret Harte, in his inimitable style, has put into exquisite verse, the story of the waiting of this true-hearted Spanish maiden[1]:

" He with grave provincial magnates long had held
    serene debate
On the Treaty of Alliance and the high affairs of state;

He from grave provincial magnates oft had turned
    to talk apart
With the Comandante's daughter on the questions
    of the heart,

---

[1] From Poems by Bret Harte. By permission of the publishers, The Houghton Mifflin Company, Boston, Mass.

Until points of gravest import yielded slowly one by
    one,
And by Love was consummated what Diplomacy
    begun;

Till beside the deep embrasures, where the brazen
    cannon are,
He received the twofold contract for approval of the
    Czar;

Till beside the brazen cannon the betrothèd bade
    adieu,
And from sallyport and gateway north the Russian
    eagles flew.

Long beside the deep embrasures, where the brazen
    cannon are,
Did they wait the promised bridegroom and the answer
    of the Czar.

Day by day . . .

Week by week . . .

So each year the seasons shifted, — wet and warm and
    drear and dry;
Half a year of clouds and flowers, half a year of dust and
    sky.

Still it brought no ship nor message, — brought no
    tidings, ill or meet,
For the statesmanlike Commander, for the daughter
    fair and sweet.

Yet she heard the varying message, voiceless to all
  ears beside:
'He will come,' the flowers whispered; 'Come no
  more,' the dry hills sighed.

.   .   .   .   .   .

Then the grim Commander, pacing where the brazen
  cannon are,
Comforted the maid with proverbs, wisdom gathered
  from afar;

.   .   .   .   .   .

So with proverbs and caresses, half in faith and half
  in doubt,
Every day some hope was kindled, flickered, faded, and
  went out.

.   .   .   .   .   .

Forty years on wall and bastion swept the hollow idle
  breeze
Since the Russian eagle fluttered from the California
  seas;

Forty years on wall and bastion wrought its slow but
  sure decay,
And St. George's cross was lifted in the port of Monterey;

And the Citadel was lighted, and the hall was gaily
  drest,
All to honor Sir George Simpson, famous traveler and
  guest.

.   .   .   .   .   .

The formal speeches ended, and amidst the laugh and
  wine,
Some one spoke of Concha's lover, — heedless of the
  warning sign.

Quickly then cried Sir George Simpson: ' Speak no ill
    of him, I pray!
He is dead. He died, poor fellow, forty years ago this
    day. —

' Died while speeding home to Russia, falling from a
    fractious horse.
Left a sweetheart, too, they tell me. Married, I
    suppose, of course!

' Lives she yet?' A deathlike silence fell on banquet,
    guests, and hall,
And a trembling figure rising fixed the awestruck gaze
    of all.

Two black eyes in darkened orbits gleamed beneath the
    nun's white hood;
Black serge hid the wasted figure, bowed and stricken
    where it stood.

' Lives she yet?' Sir George repeated. All were hushed
    as Concha drew
Closer yet her nun's attire. 'Senyor, pardon, she died,
    too!' "

In 1810 Moraga, the ensign at the presidio, was
sent with seventeen men to punish the gentiles of
the region of the Carquines Strait, who for several
years had been harassing the neophytes at San
Francisco, and sixteen of whom they had killed.
Moraga had a hard fight against a hundred and
twenty of them, and captured eighteen, whom he
soon released, " as they were all sure to die of

their wounds." The survivors retreated to their huts and made a desperate resistance, and were so determined not to be captured that, when one hut was set on fire, its inmates preferred to perish in the flames rather than to surrender. A full report of this affair was sent to the King of Spain, and as a result he promoted Moraga and other officers, and increased the pay of some of the soldiers. He also tendered the thanks of the nation to all the participants.

Runaway neophytes gave considerable trouble for several years, and in 1819 a force was sent from San Francisco to punish these recalcitrants and their allies. A sharp fight took place near the site of the present Stockton, in which 27 Indians were killed, 20 wounded, and 16 captured, with 49 horses.

The Mission report for 1821–1830 shows a decrease in neophyte population from 1252 to 219, though this was largely caused by the sending of neophytes to the newly founded Missions of San Rafael and San Francisco Solano.

San Francisco was secularized in 1834–1835, with Joaquin Estudillo as comisionado. The valuation in 1835 was real estate and fixtures, $25,800; church property, $17,800; available assets in excess of debts (chiefly live-stock), $16,400, or a total of $60,000. If any property was ever divided among the Indians, there is no record to show it.

On June 5, 1845, Pio Pico's proclamation was

made, requiring the Indians of Dolores Mission to reunite and occupy it or it would be declared abandoned and disposed of for the general good of the department. A fraudulent title to the Mission was given, and antedated February 10, 1845; but it was afterwards declared void, and the building was duly returned to the custody of the archbishop, under whose direction it still remains.

After Commodore Sloat had taken possession of Monterey for the United States, in 1846, it was merely the work of a day or so to get despatches to Captain Montgomery, of the ship " Portsmouth," who was in San Francisco bay and who immediately raised the stars and stripes, and thus the city of the Golden Gate entered into American possession. While the city was materially concerned in the events immediately following the occupation, the Mission was already too nearly dead to participate. In 1846 the bishop succeeded in finding a curate for a short period, but nothing in the records can be found as to the final disposition of the property belonging to the ex-Mission. In the political caldron it had totally disappeared.

In the early days the Mission Indians were buried in the graveyard, then the soldiers and settlers, Spanish and Mexican, and the priests, and, later, the *Americanos*. But all is neglected and uncared for, except by Nature, and, after all, perhaps it is better so. The kindly spirited

Earth Mother has given forth vines and myrtle and ivy and other plants in profusion, that have hidden the old graveled walks and the broken flags. Rose bushes grow untrimmed, untrained, and frankly beautiful; while pepper and cypress wave gracefully and poetically suggestive over graves of high and low, historic and unknown. For here are names carved on stone denoting that beneath lie buried those who helped make California history. Just at the side entrance of the church is a stone with this inscription to the first governor of California: "Aqui yacen los restos del Capitan Don Luis Antonio Argüello, Primer Gobernador del Alta California, Bajo el Gobierno Mejicano. Nació en San Francisco el 21 de Junio, 1774, y murió en el mismo lugar el 27 de Marzo, 1830."

Farther along is a brown stone monument, erected by the members of the famous fire company, to Casey, who was hung by the Vigilantes — Casey, who shot James King of William. The monument, adorned with firemen's helmets and bugles in stone, stands under the shadow of drooping pepper sprays, and is inscribed: "Sacred to the memory of James P. Casey, who Departed this life May 23, 1856, Aged 27 years. May God forgive my Persecutors. Requiescat en pace."

Poor, sad Dolores! How utterly lost it now looks!

During the earthquake and fire of 1906, the

new church by its side was destroyed. But the old Indian-built structure was preserved and still stands as a grand memorial of the past.

CHAPTER XVI

On the tragic events at San Diego that led to the delay in the founding of San Juan Capistrano I have already fully dwelt. The Mission was founded by Serra, November 1, 1776, and the adobe church recently restored by the Landmarks Club is said to be the original church built at that time.

Troubles began here early, as at San Gabriel, owing to the immorality of the guards with the Indian women, and in one disturbance three Indians were killed and several wounded. In 1781 the padre feared another uprising, owing to incitements of the Colorado River Indians, who came here across the desert and sought to arouse the local Indians to revolt.

In 1787 Governor Fages reported that San Juan was in a thoroughly prosperous condition; lands were fertile, ministers faithful and zealous, and natives well disposed. In 1800 the number of neophytes was 1046, horses and cattle 8500, while it had the vast number of 17,000 sheep. Crops were 6300 bushels, and in 1797 the presidios of Santa Barbara and San Diego owed San Juan

FACHADA OF MISSION SAN FRANCISCO.

RUINS OF MISSION SAN JUAN CAPISTRANO.

ARCHED CLOISTERS AT SAN JUAN CAPISTRANO.

Photograph by Fred W. Twogood, Riverside.
ARCHED CORRIDORS AT SAN JUAN CAPISTRANO.

Mission over $6000 for supplies furnished. In 1794 two large adobe granaries with tile roofs, and forty houses for neophytes were built. In February, 1797, work was begun on the church, the remains of which are now to be seen. It is in the form of a Roman cross, ninety feet wide and a hundred and eighty feet long, and was planned by Fray Gorgonio. It was probably the finest of all the California Mission structures. Built of quarried stone, with arched roof of the same material and a lofty tower adorning its *fachada*, it justifies the remark that "it could not be duplicated to-day under $100,000."

The consecration of the beautiful new church took place, September 7, 1806. President Tapis was aided by padres from many Missions, and the scene was made gorgeous and brilliant by the presence of Governor Arrillaga and his staff, with many soldiers from San Diego and Santa Barbara.

The following day another mass was said and sermon preached, and on the 9th the bones of Padre Vicente Fuster were transferred to their final resting-place within the altar of the new church. A solemn requiem mass was chanted, thus adding to the solemnity of the occasion.

The church itself originally had seven domes. Only two now remain. In the earthquake of 1812, when the tower fell, one of the domes was crushed, but the others remained fairly solid and intact until the sixties of the last century, when, with a zeal that outran all discretion, and that the fool-killer should have been permitted to restrain, they were blown up with gunpowder by mistaken friends who expected to rebuild the church with the same material, but never did so.

This earthquake of 1812 was felt almost the whole length of the Mission chain, and it did much damage. It occurred on Sunday morning, December 8. At San Juan a number of neophytes were at morning mass; the day had opened with intense sultriness and heaviness; the air was hot and seemed charged with electricity. Suddenly a shock was felt. All were alarmed, but, devoted to his high office, the padre began again the solemn words, when, suddenly, the second shock came and sent the great tower crashing down upon one of the domes or vaults, and in a moment the whole mass of masonry came down upon the congregation. Thirty-nine were buried in the next two days, and four were taken out of the ruins later. The officiating priest escaped, as by a miracle, through the sacristy.

It was in 1814 that Padre Boscana, who had been serving at San Luis Rey, came to reside at San Juan Capistrano, where he wrote the interesting account of the Indians that is so often quoted. In 1812 its population gained its greatest figure, 1361.

In November, 1833, Figueroa secularized the Mission by organizing a " provisional pueblo " of the Indians, and claiming that the padres voluntarily gave up the temporalities. There is no record of any inventory, and what became of the church property is not known. Lands were apportioned to the Indians by Captain Portilla. The following year, most probably, all this provisional work of Figueroa's was undone, and the Mission was secularized in the ordinary way, but in 1838 the Indians begged for the pueblo organization again, and freedom from overseers, whether lay or clerical. In 1840 Padre Zalvidea was instructed to emancipate them from Mission rule as speedily as possible. Janssens was appointed majordomo, and he reported that he zealously worked for the benefit of the Mission, repairing broken fences and ditches, bringing back runaway neophytes, clothing them and caring for the stock. But orders soon began to come in for the delivery of cattle and horses, applications rapidly came in for grants of the Mission ranches, and about the middle of June, 1841, the lands were divided among the ex-neophytes, about 100 in number, and some forty whites. At the end of July regulations were published for the foundation of the pueblo, and Don Juan Bandini soon thereafter went to supervise the work. He remained until March, 1842, in charge of the community property, and then left about half a dozen white families and twenty or more ex-neophytes duly organized as a pueblo.

In 1843 San Juan was one of the Missions the temporalities of which were to be restored to the padres, provided they paid one-eighth of all produce into the public treasury. In 1844 it was reported that San Juan had no minister, and all its neophytes were scattered. In 1845 Pico's decree was published, stating that it was to be considered a pueblo; the church, curate's house, and court-house should be reserved, and the rest of the property sold at auction for the payment of debts and the support of public worship. In December of that year the ex-Mission buildings and gardens were sold to Forster and McKinley for $710, the former of whom retained possession for many years. In 1846 the pueblo was reported as possessing a population of 113 souls.

Twenty years ago there used to be one of the best of the Mission libraries at San Juan. The books were all in old-style leather, sheepskin and parchment bindings, some of them tied with leathern thongs, and a few having heavy home-made metal clasps. They were all in Latin or Spanish, and were well known books of divinity. The first page of the record of marriages was written and signed by Junipero Serra.

There are still several interesting relics; among others, two instruments, doubtless Indian-made, used during the Easter services. One is a board studded with handle-like irons, which, when moved rapidly from side to side, makes a hideous noise. Another is a three-cornered box, on which are similar irons, and in this a loose stone is rattled. In the service called " las tinieblas," — the utter darkness, — expressive of the darkness after the

Photograph by Harold A. Parker, Pasadena.

CAMPANILE AND RUINS OF MISSION SAN JUAN CAPISTRANO.

ENTRANCE TO SAN JUAN CAPISTRANO CHAPEL.

Photograph by Fred W. Twogood, Riverside.

INNER COURT AND RUINED ARCHES, MISSION SAN JUAN CAPISTRANO.

BELLS OF MISSION SAN JUAN CAPISTRANO

crucifixion, when the church is absolutely without light, the appalling effect of these noises, heightened by the clanking of chains, is indescribable.

In proof of the tireless industry of the priests and Indians of their charge, there are to be found at San Juan many ruins of the aqueducts, or flumes, some of brick, others of wood, supported across ravines, which conveyed the water needed to irrigate the eighty acres of orchard, vineyard, and garden that used to be surrounded by an adobe wall. Reservoirs, cisterns, and zanjas of brick, stone, and cement are seen here and there, and several remnants of the masonry aqueducts are still found in the village.

CHAPTER XVII

RIVERA delayed the founding of San Francisco and Santa Clara for reasons of his own; and when, in September, 1776, he received a letter from Viceroy Bucareli, in which were references clearly showing that it was supposed by the writer that they were already established, he set to work without further delay, and went with Padre Peña, as already related. The Mission was duly founded January 12, 1777. A square of seventy yards was set off and buildings at once begun. Cattle and other Mission property were sent down from San Francisco and San Carlos, and the guard returned. But it was not long before the Indians developed an unholy love for contraband beef, and Moraga and his soldiers were sent for to capture and punish the thieves. Three of them were killed, but even then depredations occasionally continued. At the end of the year there had been sixty-seven baptisms, including eight adults, and twenty-five deaths.

The present is the third site occupied by Santa Clara. The Mission was originally established some three miles away, near Alviso, at the head-waters of the San Francisco Bay, near the river

Guadalupe, on a site called by the Indians So-co-is-u-ka (laurel wood). It was probably located there on account of its being the chief rendezvous of the Indians, fishing being good, the river having an abundance of salmon trout. The Mission remained there only a short time, as the waters rose twice in 1779, and washed it out. Then the padres removed, in 1780-1782, and built about 150 yards southwest of the present broad-gauge (Southern Pacific) depot, where quite recently traces were found of the old adobe walls. They remained at this spot, deeming the location good, until an earthquake in 1812 gave them considerable trouble. A second earthquake in 1818 so injured their buildings that they felt compelled to move to the present site, which has been occupied ever since. The Mission Church and other buildings were begun in 1818, and finally dedicated in 1822. The site was called by the Indians *Gerguensun* — the Valley of the Oaks.

On the 29th of November, 1777, the pueblo of San José was founded. The padres protested at the time that it was too near the Mission of Santa Clara, and for the next decade there was constant irritation, owing to the encroachments of the white settlers upon the lands of the Indians. Complaints were made and formally acted upon, and in July, 1801, the boundaries were surveyed, as asked for by the padres, and landmarks clearly marked and agreed upon so as to prevent future disputes.

In 1800 Santa Clara was the banner Mission for population, having 1247. Live-stock had increased to about 5000 head of each (cattle and horses), and crops were good.

In 1802, August 12, a grand high altar, which had been obtained in Mexico, was consecrated with elaborate ceremonies.

Padre Viader, the priest in charge, was a very muscular and athletic man; and one night, in 1814, a young gentile giant, named Marcelo, and two companions attacked him. In the rough and tumble fight which ensued the padre came out ahead; and after giving the culprits a severe homily on the sin of attacking a priest, they were pardoned, Marcelo becoming one of his best and most faithful friends thereafter. Robinson says Viader was " a good old man, whose heart and soul were in proportion to his immense figure."

In 1820 the neophyte population was 1357, stock 5024, horses 722, sheep 12,060. The maximum of population was reached in 1827, of 1464 souls. After that it began rapidly to decline. The crops, too, were smaller after 1820, without any apparent reason.

In 1837 secularization was effected by Ramon Estrada. In 1839-1840 reports show that two-thirds of the cattle and sheep had disappeared. The downfall of the Mission was very rapid. The neophyte population in 1832 was 1125, in 1834 about 800, and at the end of the decade about 290, with 150 more scattered in the district.

Photograph by Fred W. Twogood, Riverside.

IN THE AMBULATORY AT SAN JUAN CAPISTRANO.

Photograph by Fred W. Twogood, Riverside.

ONE OF THE DOORS, SAN JUAN CAPISTRANO.

MISSION SANTA CLARA IN 1849.

Photograph by Harold A. Parker, Pasadena.

CHURCH OF SANTA CLARA.
On the site of old Mission of Santa Clara.

The total of baptisms from 1777 to 1874 is 8640, of deaths 6950.

The old register of marriages records 3222 weddings from January 12, 1778, to August 15, 1863.

In 1833 Padre Viader closed his missionary service of nearly forty years in California by leaving the country, and Padre Francisco García Diego, the prefect of the Zacatecan friars, became his successor. Diego afterwards became the first bishop of California.

In July, 1839, a party called Yozcolos, doubtless after their leader, attacked the neophytes guarding the Santa Clara wheat-fields, killing one of them. The attackers were pursued, and their leader slain, and the placing of his head on a pole seemed to act as a deterrent of further acts for awhile.

In December of the same year Prado Mesa made an expedition against gentile thieves in the region of the Stanislaus River. He was surprised by the foe, three of his men killed, and he and six others wounded, besides losing a number of his weapons. This Indian success caused great alarm, and a regular patrol was organized to operate between San José and San Juan Missions for the protection of the ranchos. This uprising of the Indians was almost inevitable. Deprived of their maintenance at the Missions, they were practically thrown on their own resources, and in many cases this left them a prey to the evil leadership of desperate men of their own class.

Santa Clara was one of the Missions immediately affected by the decree of Michcltorena, of March 29, 1843, requiring that the padres reassume the management of the temporalities. They set to work to gather up what fragments they could find, but the flocks and herds were " lent " where they could not be recovered, and one flock of 4000 sheep — the padre says 6000 — were taken by M. J. Vallejo, " legally, in aid of the government."

Pio Pico's decree of June 5, 1845, affected Santa Clara. Andrés Pico made a valuation of the property at $16,173. There were then 130 ex-neophytes, the live-stock had dwindled down to 430 cattle, 215 horses, and 809 sheep. The padre found it necessary to write a sharp letter to the alcalde of San José on the grog-shops of that pueblo, which encouraged drinking among his Indians to such extent that they were completely demoralized.

March 19, 1851, the parish priest, who was a cultivated and learned Jesuit, and who had prepared the way, succeeded in having the Santa Clara College established in the old Mission buildings. On the 28th of April, 1855, it was chartered with all the rights and privileges of a university. In due time the college grew to large proportions, and it was found imperative either to remove the old Mission structure completely, or renovate it out of all recognition. This latter was done, so that but little of the old church remains.

In restoring it in 1861–1862 the nave was allowed to remain, but in 1885 it was found necessary to remove it. Its walls were five feet thick. The adobe bricks were thrown out upon the plaza behind the cross.

The present occupation of Santa Clara as a university as well as a church necessitated the adaptation of the old cloisters to meet the modern conditions. Therefore the casual visitor would scarcely notice that the reception-room into which he is ushered is a part of the old cloisters. The walls are about three feet thick, and are of adobe. In the garden the beams of the cloister roofs are to be seen.

The old Mission vineyard, where the grapes used to thrive, is now converted into a garden. A number of the old olive trees still remain. Of the three original bells of the Mission, two still call the faithful to worship. One was broken and had to be recast in San Francisco.

On the altar, there are angels with flambeaux in their hands, of wooden carving. These are deemed the work of the Indians. There are also several old statues of the saints, including San Joaquin, Santa Ana, San Juan Capistrano, and Santa Colette. In the sodality chapel, also, there are statues of San Francisco and San Antonio. The altar rail of the restored Santa Clara church was made from the beams of the old Mission. These were of redwood, secured from the Santa Cruz mountains, and, I believe, are the earliest specimens of redwood used for lumber in California. The rich natural coloring and the beauty of the grain and texture have improved with the years. The old octagonal pulpit, though not now used, is restored and honored, standing upon a modern pedestal.

Santa Clara was noted for the longevity of some of its Indians. One of them, Gabriel, who died in 1891 or 1892 at the hospital in Salinas, claimed he was a grandfather when Serra came in 1767. He must have been over 150 years old when he died. Another, Inigo, was known to be 101 years of age at his death.

In a room in the college building is gathered together an interesting collection of articles belonging to the old Mission. Here are the chairs of the sanctuary, processional candlesticks, pictures, and the best bound book in the State — an old choral. It rests on a stand at the end of the room. The lids are of wood, covered with thick leather and bound in very heavy bronze, with bosses half an inch high. Each corner also has bronze protuberances, half an inch long, that stand out on the bottom, or edge of the cover, so that they raise the whole book. The volume is of heaviest vellum and is entirely hand-written in red and black; and though a century or more has passed since it was written it is clear and perfect. It has 139 pages. The brothers of the college have placed this inscription over it: " Ancient choral, whose wooden cover, leather bound and covered in bronze, came, probably, originally from Spain, and has age of some 500 years."

In a case which extends across the room are ancient vestments, the key of the old Mission, statuary brackets from the ancient altar, the altar bell, crown of thorns from the Mission crucifix, altar card-frames, and the rosary and crucifix that once belonged to Padre Magin Catalá.

Padre Catalá, the good man of Santa Clara, is deemed by the leaders of the Catholic Church in California to be worthy the honors and elevation of sainthood, and proceedings are now in operation before the highest Court of the Church in Rome to see whether he is entitled to these posthumous honors. The Franciscan historian for California, Father Zephyrin Englehardt, has written a book entitled The Holy Man of Santa Clara, in which not only the life of Padre Catalá is given, but the whole of the procedure necessary to convince the Church tribunal of his worth and sainthood. The matter is not yet (1913) settled.

On the walls are some of the ancient paintings, one especially noteworthy. It is of Christ multiplying the loaves and fishes (John vi. 11). While it is not a great work of art, the benignity and sweetness of the Christ face redeem it from crudeness. With upraised right hand he is blessing the loaves which rest in his left hand, while the boy with the fishes kneels reverently at his feet.

The University of Santa Clara is now rapidly erecting its new buildings, in a modified form of

Mission architecture, tó meet its enlarging needs.
The buildings, when completed, will present to
the world a great institution of learning — the
oldest west of the Rocky Mountains — well
equipped in every department for the important
labor in the education of the Catholic youth of
California and the west that it has undertaken.

CHAPTER XVIII

For thirteen years the heart of the venerable Serra was made sick by the postponements in the founding of this Mission. The Viceroy de Croix had ordered Governor Rivera " to recruit seventy-five soldiers for the establishment of a presidio and three Missions in the channel of Santa Barbara: one towards the north of the channel, which was to be dedicated to the Immaculate Conception; one towards the south, dedicated to San Buenaventura, and a third in the centre, dedicated to Santa Barbara."

It was with intense delight that Serra received a call from Governor Neve, who, in February, 1782, informed him that he was prepared to proceed at once to the founding of the Missions of San Buenaventura and Santa Barbara. Although busy training his neophytes, he determined to go in person and perform the necessary ceremonies. Looking about for a padre to accompany him, and all his own coadjutors being engaged, he bethought him of Father Pedro Benito Cambon, a returned invalid missionary from the Philippine Islands, who was recuperating at San Diego.

He accordingly wrote Padre Cambon, requesting him, if possible, to meet him at San Gabriel. On his way to San Gabriel, Serra passed through the Indian villages of the channel region, and could not refrain from joyfully communicating ᴜᴄ news to the Indians that, very speedily, he would return to them, and establish Missions in their midst.

In the evening of March 18, Serra reached Los Angeles, and next evening, after walking to San Gabriel, weighed down with his many cares, and weary with his long walk, he still preached an excellent sermon, it being the feast of the patriarch St. Joseph. Father Cambon had arrived, and after due consultation with him and the governor, the date for the setting out of the expedition was fixed for Tuesday, March 26. The week was spent in confirmation services and other religious work, and, on the date named, after solemn mass, the party set forth. It was the most imposing procession ever witnessed in California up to that time, and called forth many gratified remarks from Serra. There were seventy soldiers, with their captain, commander for the new presidio, ensign, sergeant, and corporals. In full gubernatorial dignity followed Governor Neve, with ten soldiers of the Monterey company, their wives and families, servants and neophytes.

At midnight they halted, and a special messenger overtook them with news which led the governor to return at once to San Gabriel with his

SIDE ENTRANCE AT SAN BUENAVENTURA.

FACHADA OF MISSION SAN BUENAVENTURA.

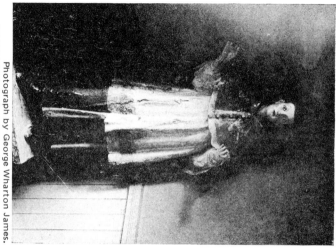

Photograph by George Wharton James.

STATUE OF SAN BUENAVENTURA.

Now at Dominican Convent, Mission San Jose.

Photograph by Harold A. Parker, Pasadena.

RAWHIDE FASTENING OF MISSION BELL, AND
WORM-EATEN BEAM.

ten soldiers. He ordered the procession to proceed, however, found the San Buenaventura Mission, and there await his arrival. Serra accordingly went forward, and on the twenty-ninth arrived at "Assumpta." Here, the next day, on the feast of Easter, they pitched their tents, " erected a large cross, and prepared an altar under a shade of evergreens," where the venerable Serra, now soon to close his life-work, blessed the cross and the place, solemnized mass, preached a sermon to the soldiers on the Resurrection of Christ, and formally dedicated the Mission to God, and placed it under the patronage of St. Joseph.

In the earlier part of the last century the Mission began to grow rapidly. Padres Francisco Dumetz and Vicente de Santa María, who had been placed in charge of the Mission from the first, were gladdened by many accessions, and the Mission flocks and herds also increased rapidly. Indeed, we are told that " in 1802 San Buenaventura possessed finer herds of cattle and richer fields of grain than any of her contemporaries, and her gardens and orchards were visions of wealth and beauty."

On his second visit to the California coast, Vancouver, when anchored off Santa Barbara, traded with Padre Santa María of San Buenaventura for a flock of sheep and as many vegetables as twenty mules could carry.

It is to Vancouver, on this voyage, that we owe the names of a number of points on the California coast, as, for instance, Points Sal, Argüello, Felipe, Vicente, Dumetz, Fermin, and Lasuen.

In 1795 there was a fight between the neophyte and gentile Indians, the former killing two chiefs and taking captive several of the latter. The leaders on both sides were punished, the neophyte Domingo even being sentenced to work in chains.

In 1806 the venerable Santa María, one of the Mission founders, died. His remains were ultimately placed in the new church.

In 1800 the largest population in its history was reached, with 1297 souls. Cattle and horses prospered, and the crops were reported as among the best in California.

The earthquake of 1812–1813 did considerable damage at San Buenaventura. Afraid lest the sea would swallow them up, the people fled to San Joaquin y Santa Ana for three months, where a temporary *jacal* church was erected. The tower and a part of the *fachada* had to be torn down and rebuilt, and this was done by 1818, with a new chapel dedicated to San Miguel in addition.

That San Buenaventura was prosperous is shown by the fact that in June, 1820, the government owed it $27,385 for supplies, $6200 in stipends, and $1585 for a cargo of hemp, — a total of $35,170, which, says Bancroft, " there was not the slightest chance of it ever receiving."

In 1823 the president and vice-prefect Señan,

who had served as padre at this Mission for twenty-five years, died August 24, and was buried by the side of Santa María. After his death San Buenaventura began rapidly to decline.

In 1822 a neophyte killed his wife for adultery. It is interesting to note that in presenting his case the fiscal said that as the culprit had been a Christian only seven years, and was yet ignorant in matters of domestic discipline, he asked for the penalty of five years in the chain gang and then banishment.

The baptisms for the whole period of the Mission's history, viz., for 1782–1834, are 3876. There is still preserved at the Mission the first register, which was closed in 1809. At that time 2648 baptisms had been administered. The padre presidente, Serra, wrote the heading for the Index, and the contents themselves were written in a beautiful hand by Padre Señan. There are four signatures which occur throughout in the following order: Pedro Benito Cambon, Francisco Dumetz, Vicente de Sta María, and José Señan.

The largest population was 1330 in 1816. The largest number of cattle was 23,400 in the same year. In 1814, 4652 horses; in 1816, 13,144 sheep.

Micheltorena's decree in 1843 restored the temporalities of the Mission to the padres. This was one of the two Missions, Santa Inés being the other, that was able to provide a moderate subsistence out of the wreck left by secularization.

On the 5th of December, 1845, Pico rénted San Buenaventura to José Arnaz and Marcisco Botello for $1630 a year. There are no statistics of the value of the property after 1842, though in April of 1843 Padre Jimeno reports 2382 cattle, 529 horses, 2299 sheep, 220 mules and 18 asses, 1032 fruit trees and 11,907 vines. In November of that same year the bishop appointed Presbyter, Rosales, since which time the Mission has been the regular parish church of the city.

In 1893 the Mission church was renovated out of all its historic association and value by Father Rubio, who had a good-natured but fearfully destructive zeal for the " restoration " of the old Missions. Almost everything has been modernized. The fine old pulpit, one of the richest treasures of the Mission, was there several years ago; but when, in 1904, I inquired of the then pastor where it was, I was curtly informed that he neither knew nor cared. All the outbuildings have been demolished and removed in order to make way for the modern spirit of commercialism which in the last decade has struck the town. It is now an ordinary church, with little but its history to redeem it from the look of smug modernity which is the curse of the present age.

Before leaving San Buenaventura it may be interesting to note that a few years ago I was asked about two " wooden bells " which were said to have been hung in the tower at this Mission. I deemed the question absurd, but on one of my visits found one of these bells in a storeroom under the altar, and another still hanging in the belfry. By whom, or why, these dummy bells were made, I have not been able to discover.

CHAPTER XIX

AFTER the founding of San Buenaventura. Governor Neve arrived from San Gabriel, inspected the new site, and expressed himself as pleased with all that had been done. A few days later he, with Padre Serra, and a number of soldiers and officers, started up the coast, and, selecting a site known to the Indians after the name of their chief, *Yanonalit*, established the presidio of Santa Barbara. Yanonalit was very friendly, and as he had authority over thirteen rancherías he was able to help matters along easily. This was April 21, 1782.

When Serra came to the establishment of the presidio, he expected also to found the Mission, and great was his disappointment. This undoubtedly hastened his death, which occurred August 28, 1782.

It was not until two years later that Neve's successor, Fages, authorized Serra's successor, Lasuen, to proceed. Even then it was feared that he would demand adherence to new conditions which were to the effect that the padres should not have control over the temporal affairs of the Indians;

MISSION SANTA BARBARA.

Photograph by Howard Tibbitts, San Francisco.

MISSION SANTA BARBARA FROM THE HILLSIDE.

INTERIOR OF MISSION SANTA BARBARA.

but, as the guardian of the college had positively refused to send missionaries for the new establishments, unless they were founded on the old lines, Fages tacitly agreed. On December 4, therefore, the cross was raised on the site called *Taynayan* by the Indians and *Pedragoso* by the Spaniards, and formal possession taken, though the first mass was not said until Fages's arrival on the 16th. Lasuen was assisted by Padres Antonio Paterna and Cristobal Oramas. Father Zephyrin has written a very interesting account of Santa Barbara Mission, some of which is as follows:

" The work of erecting the necessary buildings began early in 1787. With a number of Indians, who had first to be initiated into the mysteries of house construction, Fathers Paterna and Oramas built a dwelling for themselves together with a chapel. These were followed by a house for the servants, who were male Indians, a granary, carpenter shop, and quarters for girls and unmarried young women.

" In succeeding years other structures arose on the rocky height as the converts increased and industries were introduced. At the end of 1807 the Indian village, which had sprung up just southwest of the main building, consisted of 252 separate adobe dwellings harboring as many Indian families. The present Mission building, with its fine corridor, was completed about the close of the eighteenth century. The fountain in front arose in 1808. It furnished the water for the great basin just below, which served for the general laundry purposes of the Indian village. The water was led through earthen pipes from the reservoir north of the church, which to this day furnishes Santa Barbara with water. It was built in 1806. To obtain the precious liquid from the mountains, a very strong dam was built across ' Pedragoso ' creek about two miles back of the Mission. It is still in good condition. Then there were various structures scattered far and near for the different trades, since everything that was used in the way of clothing and food had to be raised or manufactured at the Mission.

" The chapel grew too small within a year from the time it was dedicated, Sunday, May 21, 1787. It was therefore enlarged in 1788, but by the year 1792 this, also, proved too small. Converts were coming in rapidly. The old structure was then taken down, and a magnificent edifice took its place in 1793. Its size was 25 by 125 feet. There were three small chapels on each side, like the two that are attached to the present church. An earthquake, which occurred on Monday, December 21, 1812, damaged this adobe building to such an extent that it had to be taken down. On its site rose the splendid structure, which is still the admiration of the traveler. Padre Antonio Ripoll superintended the work, which continued through five years, from 1815 to 1820. It was dedicated on the 10th of September, 1820. The walls, which are six feet thick, consist of irregular sandstone blocks, and are further strengthened by solid stone buttresses measuring nine by nine feet. The towers to a height of thirty feet are a solid mass of stone and cement twenty feet square. A narrow passage leads through one of these to the top, where the old bells still call the faithful to service as of yore. Doubtless the Santa Barbara Mission church is the most solid structure of

its kind in California. It is 165 feet long, forty feet
wide and thirty feet high on the outside. Like the
monastery, the church is roofed with tiles which were
manufactured at the Mission by the Indians."

The report for 1800 is full of interest. It re-
counts the activity in building, tells of the death
of Padre Paterna, who died in 1793, and was followed by Estévan Tapis (afterwards padre presidente), and says that 1237 natives have been baptized, and that the Mission now owns 2492 horses
and cattle, and 5615 sheep. Sixty neophytes
are engaged in weaving and allied tasks; the
carpenter of the presidio is engaged at a dollar
a day to teach the neophytes his trade; and a
corporal is teaching them tanning at $150 a year.

In 1803 the population was the highest the
Mission ever reached, with 1792. In May, 1808,
a determined effort lasting nine days was made to
rid the region of ground squirrels, and about a
thousand were killed.

The earthquakes of 1812 alarmed the people
and damaged the buildings at Santa Barbara as
elsewhere. The sea was much disturbed, and
new springs of asphaltum were formed, great
cracks opened in the mountains, and the population fled all buildings and lived in the open air.

On the sixth of December, in the same year, the
arrival of Bouchard, "the pirate," gave them a new
shock of terror. The padres had already been
warned to send all their valuables to Santa Inés,

and the women and children were to proceed
thither on the first warning of an expected attack.
But Bouchard made no attack. He merely
wanted to exchange "prisoners." He played a
pretty trick on the Santa Barbara comandante
in negotiating for such exchange, and then, when
the hour of delivery came, it was found he had but
one prisoner, — a poor drunken wretch whom the
authorities would have been glad to get rid of at
any price.

In 1824 the Indian revolt, which is fully treated
in the chapters on Santa Inés and Purísima,
reached Santa Barbara. While Padre Ripoll
was absent at the presidio, the neophytes armed
themselves and worked themselves into a frenzy.
They claimed that they were in danger from the
Santa Inés rebels unless they joined the revolt,
though they promised to do no harm if only the
soldiers were sent and kept away. Accordingly
Ripoll gave an order for the guard to withdraw,
but the Indians insisted that the soldiers leave
their weapons. Two refused, whereupon they
were savagely attacked and wounded. This so
incensed Guerra that he marched up from the
presidio in full force, and a fight of several hours
ensued, the Indians shooting with guns and arrows
from behind the pillars of the corridors. Two
Indians were killed and three wounded, and four
of the soldiers were wounded. When Guerra
retired to the presidio, the Indians stole all the
clothing and other portable property they could

carry (carefully respecting everything, however, belonging to the church), and fled to the hills. That same afternoon the troops returned and, despite the padre's protest, sacked the Indians' houses and killed all the stragglers they found, regardless of their guilt or innocence. The Indians refused to return, and retreated further over the mountains to the recesses of the Tulares. Here they were joined by escaped neophytes from San Fernando and other Missions. The alarm spread to San Buenaventura and San Gabriel, but few, if any, Indians ran away. In the meantime the revolt was quelled at Santa Inés and Purísima, as elsewhere recorded.

On the strength of reports that he heard, Governor Argüello recalled the Monterey troops; but this appeared to be a mistake, for, immediately, Guerra of Santa Barbara sent eighty men over to San Emigdio, where, on April 9 and 11, severe conflicts took place, with four Indians killed, and wounded on both sides. A wind and dust storm arising, the troops returned to Santa Barbara.

In May the governor again took action, sending Captain Portilla with a force of 130 men. The prefect Sarría and Padre Ripoll went along to make as peaceable terms as possible, and a message which Sarría sent on ahead doubtless led the insurgents to sue for peace. They said they were heartily sorry for their actions and were anxious to return to Mission life, but hesitated about laying down their arms for fear of summary punishment. The gentiles still fomented trouble by working on the fears of the neophytes, but owing to Argüello's granting a general pardon, they were finally, in June, induced to return, and the revolt was at an end.

After these troubles, however, the Mission declined rapidly in prosperity. Though the buildings under Padre Ripoll were in excellent condition, and the manufacturing industries were well kept up, everything else suffered.

In 1817 a girls' school for whites was started at the presidio of Santa Barbara, but nothing further is known of it. Several years later a school was opened, and Diego Fernandez received $15 a month as its teacher. But Governor Echeandía ordered that, as not a single scholar attended, this expense be discontinued; yet he required the comandante to compel parents to send their children to school.

In 1833 Presidente Duran, discussing with Governor Figueroa the question of secularization, deprecated too sudden action, and suggested a partial and experimental change at some of the oldest Missions, Santa Barbara among the number.

When the decree from Mexico, came, however, this was one of the first ten Missions to be affected thereby. Anastasio Carrillo was appointed comisionado, and acted from September, 1833. His inventory in March, 1834, showed credits, $14,953; buildings, $22,936; furniture, tools, goods in storehouse, vineyards, orchards, corrals, and animals, $19,590; church, $16,000; sacristy, $1500; church ornaments, etc., $4576; library, $152; ranchos, $30,961; total, $113,960, with a debt to be deducted of $1000.

The statistics from 1786 to 1834, the whole period of the Mission's history, show that there were 5679 baptisms, 1524 marriages, 4046 deaths. The largest population was 1792 in 1803. The largest number of cattle was 5200 in 1809, of sheep, 11,066 in 1804.

Here, as elsewhere, the comisionados found serious fault with the pueblo grog-shops. In 1837 Carrillo reports that he has broken up a place where Manuel Gonzalez sold liquor to the Indians, and he calls upon the comandante to suppress other places. In March, 1838, he complains that the troops are killing the Mission cattle, but is told that General Castro had authorized the officers to kill all the cattle needed without asking permission. When the Visitador Hartwell was here in 1839 he found Carrillo's successor Cota an unfit man, and so reported him. He finally suspended him, and the Indians became more contented and industrious under Padre Duran's supervision, though the latter refused to undertake the temporal management of affairs.

Micheltorena's decree of 1843 affected Santa Barbara, in that it was ordered returned to the control of the padres; but in the following year Padre Duran reported that it had the greatest difficulty in supporting its 287 souls. Pico's decree in 1845 retained the principal building for the bishop and padres; but all the rest and the orchards and lands were to be rented, which was accordingly done December 5, to Nicholas A. Den and Daniel Hill for $1200 per year, the property being valued at $20,288. Padre Duran was growing old, and the Indians were becoming more careless and improvident; so, when Pico wrote him to give up the Mission lands and property to the renters, he did so willingly, though he stated that the estate owed him $1000 for money he had advanced for the use of the Indians. The Indians were to receive one third of the rental, but there is no record of a cent of it ever getting into their hands. June 10, 1846, Pico sold the Mission to Richard S. Den for $7500, though the lessees seem to have kept possession until about the end of 1848. The land commission confirmed Den's title, though the evidences are that it was annulled in later litigation. Padre Duran died here early in 1846, a month after Bishop Diego. Padre Gonzalez Rubio still remained for almost thirty years longer to become the last of the old missionaries.

In 1853 a petition was presented to Rome, and Santa Barbara was erected into a Hospice, as the beginning of an Apostolic College for the education of Franciscan novitiates who are to go forth, wherever sent, as missionaries. St. Anthony's College, the modern building near by, was founded

MISSION BELL AT SANTA BARBARA.

DOOR INTO CEMETERY, SANTA BARBARA.

THE SACRISTY WALL, GARDEN AND TOWERS, MISSION SANTA BARBARA.

FACHADA OF MISSION LA PURISIMA CONCEPCION, NEAR LOMPOC, CALIF.

by the energy of Father Peter Wallischeck. It is for the education of aspirants to the Franciscan Order. There are now thirty-five students.

Five of the early missionaries and three of later date are buried in the crypt, under the floor of the sanctuary, in front of the high altar; and Bishop Diego rests under the floor at the right-hand side of the altar.

The small cemetery, which is walled in and entered from the church, is said to contain the bodies of 4000 Indians, as well as a number of whites. In the northeast corner is the vault in which are buried the members of the Franciscan community.

In the bell tower are two old bells made in 1818, as is evidenced by their inscriptions, which read alike, as follows: " Manvel Vargas me fecit ano d. 1818 Mision de Santa Barbara De la nveba California " — " Manuel Vargas made me Anno Domini 1818. Mission of Santa Barbara of New California." The first bell is fastened to its beam with rawhide thongs; the second, with a framework of iron. Higher up is a modern bell which is rung (the old ones being tolled only).

The Mission buildings surround the garden, into which no woman, save a reigning queen or the wife of the President of the United States, is allowed to enter. An exception was made in the case of the Princess Louise when her husband was the Governor-general of Canada. The wife of President Harrison also has entered. The garden, with its fine Italian cypress, planted by Bishop Diego about 1842, and its hundred varieties of semi-tropical flowers, in the center of which is a fountain where goldfish play, affords a delightful place of study, quiet, and meditation for the Franciscans.

It is well that the visitor should know that this old Mission, never so abandoned and abused as the others, has been kept up in late years entirely by the funds given to the Franciscan missionaries, who are now its custodians, and it has no other income.

The Mission Library contains a large number of valuable old books gathered from the other Missions at the time of secularization. There are also kept here a large number of the old records from which Bancroft gained much of his Mission intelligence, and which, recently, have been carefully restudied by Father Zephyrin, the California historian of the Franciscan Order. Father Zephyrin is a devoted student, and many results of his zeal and kindness are placed before my readers in this volume, owing to his generosity. His completed history of the Missions and Missionaries of California is a monumental work.

CHAPTER XX

ALTHOUGH the date of the founding of this Mission is given as December 8, 1787, — for that was the day on which Presidente Lasuen raised the cross, blessed the site, celebrated mass, and preached a dedicatory sermon, — there was no work done for several months, owing to the coming of the rainy season. In the middle of March, 1788, Sergeant Cota of Santa Barbara, with a band of laborers and an escort, went up to prepare the necessary buildings; and early in April Lasuen, accompanied by Padres Vicente Fuster and José Arroita, followed. As early as August the roll showed an acquisition of seventy-nine neophytes. During the first decade nearly a thousand baptisms were recorded, and the Mission flourished in all departments. Large crops of wheat and grain were raised, and live-stock increased rapidly. In 1804 the population numbered 1522, the highest on record during its history, and in 1810 the number of live-stock reported was over 20,000; but the unusual prosperity that attended this Mission during its earlier years was interrupted by a series of exceptional misfortunes.

The first church erected was crude and unstable, and fell rapidly into decay. Scarcely a dozen years had passed, when it became necessary to build a new one. This was constructed of adobe and roofed with tile. It was completed in 1802, but although well built, it was totally destroyed by an earthquake, as we shall see later on.

The Indians of this section were remarkably intelligent as well as diligent, and during the first years of the Mission there were over fifty rancherías in the district. According to the report of Padre Payeras in 1810, they were docile and industrious. This indefatigable worker, with the assistance of interpreters, prepared a Catechism and Manual of Confession in the native language, which he found very useful in imparting religious instruction and in uprooting the prevailing idolatry. In a little over twenty years the entire population for many leagues had been baptized, and were numbered among the converts.

This period of peace and prosperity was followed by sudden disaster. The earthquake of 1812, already noted as the most severe ever known on the Pacific Coast, brought devastation to Purísima. The morning of December 21 found padres and Indians rejoicing in the possession of the fruits of their labor of years, — a fine church, many Mission buildings, and a hundred houses built of adobe and occupied by the natives. A few hours afterward little was left that was fit for even temporary use. The first vibration, lasting four min-

utes, damaged the walls of the church. The second
shock, a half-hour later, caused the total collapse
of nearly all the buildings. Padre Payeras reported that "the earth opened in several places,
emitting water and black sand." This calamity
was quickly followed by torrents of rain, and the
ensuing floods added to the distress of the home-
less inhabitants. The remains of this old Mission
of 1802 are still to be seen near Lompoc, and on
the hillside above is a deep scar made by the earthquake, this doubtless being the crack described
by Padre Payeras. But nothing could daunt
the courage or quench the zeal of the missionaries.
Rude huts were erected for immediate needs, and,
having selected a new and more advantageous
site — five or six miles away — across the river,
they obtained the necessary permission from the
presidente, and at once commenced the construction of a new church, and all the buildings needed
for carrying on the Mission. Water for irrigation and domestic purposes was brought in cement
pipes, made and laid under the direction of the
padres, from Salsperde Creek, three miles away.
But other misfortunes were in store for these un-
lucky people. During a drought in the winter
of 1816–1817, hundreds of sheep perished for
lack of feed, and in 1818 nearly all the neophytes'
houses were destroyed by fire.

In 1823 the Mission lost one of its best friends
in the death of Padre Payeras. Had he lived another year it is quite possible his skill in adjusting

difficulties might have warded off the outbreak
that occurred among the Indians, — the famous
revolt of 1824.

This revolt, which also affected Santa Inés
and Santa Barbara (see their respective chapters),
had serious consequences at Purísima. After
the attack at Santa Inés the rebels fled to Purísima. In the meantime the neophytes at this
latter Mission, hearing of the uprising, had seized
the buildings. The guard consisted of Corporal
Tapia with four or five men. He bravely defended
the padres and the soldiers' families through the
night, but surrendered when his powder gave out.
One woman was wounded. The rebels then sent
Padres Ordaz and Tapia to Santa Inés to warn
Sergeant Carrillo not to come or the families
would be killed. Before an answer was received,
the soldiers and their families were permitted to
retire to Santa Inés, while Padre Rodriguez remained, the Indians being kindly disposed towards
him. Four white men were killed in the fight, and
seven Indians.

Left now to themselves, and knowing that they
were sure to be attacked ere long, the Indians
began to prepare for defense. They erected pali-
sades, cut loopholes in the walls of the church and
other buildings, and mounted one or two rusty
old cannon. For nearly a month they were not
molested. This was the end of February.

In the meantime the governor was getting a
force ready at Monterey to send to unite with

one under Guerra from Santa Barbara. On
March 16 they were to have met, but owing
to some mischance, the northern force had to
make the attack alone. Cavalry skirmishers were
sent right and left to cut off retreat, and the rest
of the force began to fire on the adobe walls from
muskets and a four-pounder. The four hundred
neophytes within responded with yells of defiance
and cannon, swivel-guns, and muskets, as well
as a cloud of arrows. In their inexperienced hands,
however, little damage was done with the cannon.
By and by the Indians attempted to fly, but were
prevented by the cavalry. Now realizing their
defeat, they begged Padre Rodriguez to inter-
cede for them, which he did. In two hours and a
half the conflict was over, three Spaniards being
wounded, one fatally, while there were sixteen
Indians killed and a large number wounded. As
the governor had delegated authority to the officers
to summarily dispense justice, they condemned
seven of the Indians to death for the murder of
the white men in the first conflict. They were
shot before the end of the month. Four of the
revolt ringleaders were sentenced to ten years of
labor at the presidio and then perpetual exile,
while eight others were condemned to the presidio
for eight years.

There was dissatisfaction expressed with the
penalties, — on the side of the padres by Ripoll
of Santa Barbara, who claimed that a general
pardon had been promised; and on the part of the

governor, who thought his officers had been too lenient.

An increased guard was left at Purísima after this affair, and it took some little time before the Indians completely settled down again, as it was known that the Santa Barbara Indians were still in revolt.

During all the years when contending with the destructive forces of earthquake, fire, flood, and battle, to say nothing of those foes of agriculture, — drought, frost, grasshoppers, and squirrels, — the material results of native labor were notable. In 1819 they produced about 100,000 pounds of tallow. In 1821 the crops of wheat, barley, and corn amounted to nearly 8000 bushels. Between 1822 and 1827 they furnished the presidio with supplies valued at $12,921. The population, however, gradually decreased until about 400 were left at the time of secularization in 1835. The Purísima estate at this time was estimated by the appraisers to be worth about $60,000. The inventory included a library valued at $655 and five bells worth $1000. With the exception of the church property this estate, or what remained of it, was sold in 1845 for $1110. Under the management of administrators appointed by the government, the Mission property rapidly disappeared, lands were sold, live-stock killed and scattered, and only the fragments of wreckage remained to be turned over to the jurisdiction of the padres according to the decree of Micheltorena in 1843.

The following year an epidemic of smallpox caused
the death of the greater proportion of Indians still
living at Purísima, and the final act in the history
of the once flourishing Mission was reached in
1845, when, by order of Governor Pico, the ruined
estate was sold to John Temple for the paltry
amount stated above.

In regard to its present ownership and condition, a gentleman interested writes:

"The abandoned Mission is on ground which now
belongs to the Union Oil Company of California. The
building itself has been desecrated and damaged by the
public ever since its abandonment. Its visitors apparently did not scruple to deface it in every possible
way, and what could not be stolen was ruthlessly
destroyed. It apparently was a pleasure to them to
pry the massive roof-beams loose, in order to enjoy the
crash occasioned by the breaking of the valuable tile.

"On top of this the late series of earthquakes in that
section threw down many of the brick pillars, and twisted
the remainder so badly that the front of the building
is a veritable wreck. During these earthquakes,
which lasted several weeks, tile which could not be
replaced for a thousand dollars were displaced and
broken. To save the balance of the tile, as well as
to avoid possible accidents to visitors, the secretary
of the Oil Company had the remaining tile removed
from the roof and piled up near the building for
safety."

CHAPTER XXI

Lasuen found matters far easier for him in the founding of Missions than did Serra in his later years. The viceroy agreed to pay $1000 each for the expenses of the Missions of Santa Cruz and La Soledad, and $200 each for the traveling expenses of the four missionaries needed. April 1, 1790, the guardian sent provisions and tools for Santa Cruz to the value of $1021. Lasuen delayed the founding for awhile, however, as the needful church ornaments were not at hand; but as the viceroy promised them and ordered him to go ahead by borrowing the needed articles from the other Missions, Lasuen proceeded to the founding, as I have already related.

At the end of the year 1791 the neophytes numbered 84. In 1796 the highest mark was reached with 523. In 1800 there were but 492. Up to the end of that year there had been 949 baptisms, 271 couples married, and 477 buried. There were 2354 head of large stock, and 2083 small. In 1792 the agricultural products were about 650 bushels, as against 4300 in 1800.

The corner-stone of the church was laid February 27, 1793, and was completed and formally

RUINS OF MISSION LA PURISMA CONCEPCION.

MISSION SANTA CRUZ.

RUINED WALLS OF MISSION LA SOLEDAD.

dedicated May 10, 1794, by Padre Peña from Santa Clara, aided by five other priests. Ensign Sal was present as godfather, and duly received the keys. The neophytes, servants, and troops looked on at the ceremonies with unusual interest, and the next day filled the church at the saying of the first mass. The church was about thirty by one hundred and twelve feet and twenty-five feet high. The foundation walls to the height of three feet were of stone, the front was of masonry, and the rest of adobes. The other buildings were slowly erected, and in the autumn of 1796 a flouring-mill was built and running. It was sadly damaged, however, by the December rains. Artisans were sent to build the mill and instruct the natives, and later a smith and a miller were sent to start it.

In 1798 the padre wrote very discouragingly. The establishment of the villa or town of Branci-fort, across the river, was not pleasing. A hundred and thirty-eight neophytes also had deserted, ninety of whom were afterwards brought in by Corporal Mesa. It had long been the intention of the government to found more pueblos or towns, as well as Missions in California, the former for the purpose of properly colonizing the country. Governor Borica made some personal explorations, and of three suggested sites finally chose that just across the river Lorenzo from Santa Cruz. May 12, 1797, certain settlers who had been recruited in Guadalajara arrived in a pitiable condition at Monterey; and soon thereafter they were sent to the new site under the direction of Comisionado Moraga, who was authorized to erect temporary shelters for them. August 12 the superintendent of the formal foundation, Córdoba, had all the surveying accomplished, part of an irrigating canal dug, and temporary houses partially erected. In August, after the viceroy had seen the estimated cost of the establishment, further progress was arrested by want of funds. Before the end of the century everybody concerned had come to the conclusion that the villa of Brancifort was a great blunder, — the " settlers are a scandal to the country by their immorality. They detest their exile, and render no service."

In the meantime the Mission authorities protested vigorously against the new settlement. It was located on the pasture grounds of the Indians; the laws allowed the Missions a league in every direction, and trouble would surely result. But the governor retorted, defending his choice of a site, and claiming that the neophytes were dying off, there were no more pagans to convert, and the neophytes already had more land and raised more grain than they could attend to.

In 1805 Captain Goycoechea recommended that as there were no more gentiles, the neophytes be divided between the Missions of Santa Clara and San Juan, and the missionaries sent to new fields. Of course nothing came of this.

In the decade 1820–1830 population declined rapidly, though in live-stock the Mission about held its own, and in agriculture actually increased. In 1823, however, there was another attempt to suppress it, and this doubtless came from the conflicts between the villa of Brancifort and the Mission. The effort, like the former one, was unsuccessful.

In 1834–1835 Ignacio del Valle acted as comisionado, and put in effect the order of secularization. His valuation of the property was $47,000, exclusive of land and church property, besides $10,000 distributed to the Indians. There were no subsequent distributions, yet the property disappeared, for, in 1839, when Visitador Hartwell went to Santa Cruz, he found only about one-sixth of the live-stock of the inventory of four years before. The neophytes were organized into a pueblo named Figueroa after the governor; but it was a mere organization in name, and the condition of the ex-Mission was no different from that of any of the others.

The statistics for the whole period of the Mission's existence, 1791–1834, are: baptisms, 2466; marriages, 847; deaths, 2035. The largest population was 644 in 1798. The largest number of cattle was 3700 in 1828; horses, 900, in the same year; mules, 92, in 1805; sheep, 8300, in 1826.

In January, 1840, the tower fell, and a number of tiles were carried off, a kind of premonition of the final disaster of 1851, when the walls fell, and treasure seekers completed the work of demolition.

The community of the Mission was completely broken up in 1841–1842, everything being regarded, henceforth, as part of Brancifort. In 1845 the lands, buildings, and fruit trees of the ex-Mission were valued at less than $1000, and only about forty Indians were known to remain. The Mission has now entirely disappeared.

CHAPTER XXII

LA SOLEDAD

The Mission of "Our Lady of Solitude" has only a brief record in written history; but the little that is known and the present condition of the ruins suggest much that has never been recorded.

Early in 1791 Padre Lasuen, who was searching for suitable locations for two new Missions, arrived at a point midway between San Antonio and Santa Clara. With quick perception he recognized the advantages of Soledad, known to the Indians as *Chuttusgelis*. The name of this region, bestowed by Crespí years previous, was suggestive of its solitude and dreariness; but the wide, vacant fields indicated good pasturage in seasons favored with much rain, and the possibility of securing water for irrigation promised crops from the arid lands. Lasuen immediately selected the most advantageous site for the new Mission, but several months elapsed before circumstances permitted the erection of the first rude structures.

On October ninth the Mission was finally established.

There were comparatively few Indians in that immediate region, and only eleven converts were reported as the result of the efforts of the first year. There was ample room for flocks and herds, and although the soil was not of the best and much irrigation was necessary to produce good crops, the padres with their persistent labors gradually increased their possessions and the number of their neophytes. At the close of the ninth year there were 512 Indians living at the Mission, and their property included a thousand cattle, several thousand sheep, and a good supply of horses. Five years later (in 1805) there were 727 neophytes, in spite of the fact that a severe epidemic a few years previously had reduced their numbers and caused many to flee from the Mission in fear. A new church was begun in 1808.

On July 24, 1814, Governor Arrillaga, who had been taken seriously ill while on a tour of inspection, and had hurried to Soledad to be under the care of his old friend, Padre Ibañez, died there, and was buried, July 26, under the center of the church.

For about forty years priests and natives lived a quiet, peaceful life in this secluded valley, with an abundance of food and comfortable shelter. That they were blessed with plenty and prosperity is evidenced by the record that in 1829 they furnished $1150 to the Monterey presidio. At one time they possessed over six thousand cattle; and in 1821 the number of cattle, sheep, horses, and other animals was estimated at over sixteen thousand.

After the changes brought about by political

Photograph by Howard Tibbitts, San Francisco.
ANOTHER VIEW OF THE WALLS OF MISSION LA SOLEDAD.

MISSION SAN JOSE, SOON AFTER THE DECREE OF SECULARIZATION.
From an old print.

FIGURE OF CHRIST, MISSION SAN JOSE ORPHANAGE.

administration the number of Indians rapidly decreased, and the property acquired by their united toil quickly dwindled away, until little was left but poverty and suffering.

At the time secularization was effected in 1835, according to the inventory made, the estate, aside from church property, was valued at $36,000. Six years after secular authorities took charge only about 70 Indians remained, with 45 cattle, 25 horses, and 865 sheep, — and a large debt had been incurred. On June 4, 1846, the Soledad Mission was sold to Feliciano Soveranes for $800.

One of the pitiful cases that occurred during the decline of the Missions was the death of Padre Sarría, which took place at Soledad in 1835, or, as some authorities state, in 1838. This venerable priest had been very prominent in missionary labors, having occupied the position of *Comisario Prefecto* during many years. He was also the presidente for several years. As a loyal Spaniard he declined to take the oath of allegiance to the Mexican Republic, and was nominally under arrest for about five years, or subject to exile; but so greatly was he revered and trusted as a man of integrity and as a business manager of great ability that the order of exile was never enforced. The last years of his life were spent at the Mission of Our Lady of Solitude. When devastation began and the temporal prosperity of the Mission quickly declined, this faithful pastor of a fast thinning flock refused to leave the few poverty-stricken

Indians who still sought to prolong life in their old home. One Sunday morning, while saying mass in the little church, the enfeebled and aged padre fell before the altar and immediately expired. As it had been reported that he was " leading a hermit's life and destitute of means," it was commonly believed that this worthy and devoted missionary was exhausted from lack of proper food, and in reality died of starvation.

There were still a few Indians at Soledad in 1850, their scattered huts being all that remained of the once large rancherías that existed here.

The ruins of Soledad are about four miles from the station of the Southern Pacific of that name. The church itself is at the southwest corner of a mass of ruins. These are all of adobe, though the foundations are of rough rock. Flint pebbles have been mixed with the adobe of the church walls. They were originally about three feet thick, and plastered. A little of the plaster still remains.

In 1904 there was but one circular arch remaining in all the ruins; everything else had fallen in. The roof fell in thirty years ago. At the eastern end, where the arch is, there are three or four rotten beams still in place; and on the south side of the ruins, where one line of corridors ran, a few poles still remain. Heaps of ruined tiles lie here and there, just as they fell when the supporting poles rotted and gave way.

It is claimed by the Soberanes family in Soledad

that the present ruins of the church are of the building erected about 1850 by their grandfather. The family lived in a house just southwest of the Mission, and there this grandfather was born. He was baptized, confirmed, and married in the old church, and when, after secularization, the Mission property was offered for sale, he purchased it. As the church — in the years of pitiful struggle for possession of its temporalities — had been allowed to go to ruin, this true son of the Church erected the building, the ruins of which now bring sadness to the hearts of all who care for the Missions.

CHAPTER XXIII

SAN JOSÉ DE GUADALUPE

THERE was a period of rest after the founding of Santa Cruz and La Soledad. Padre Presidente Lasuen was making ready for a new and great effort. Hitherto the Mission establishments had been isolated units of civilization, each one alone in its work save for the occasional visits of governor, inspector, or presidente. Now they were to be linked together, by the founding of intermediate Missions, into one great chain, near enough for mutual help and encouragement, the boundary of one practically the boundary of the next one, both north and south. The two new foundations of Santa Cruz and Soledad were a step in this direction, but now the plan was to be completed. With the viceroy's approval, Governor Borica authorized Lasuen to have the regions between the old Missions carefully explored for new sites. Accordingly the padres and their guards were sent out, and simultaneously such a work of investigation began as was never before known. Reports were sent in, and finally, after a careful study of the whole situation, it was concluded that five new Missions could be established and a great annual saving thereby made in future yearly expenses. Governor Borica's idea was that the new Missions would convert all the gentile Indians west of the Coast Range. This done, the guards could be reduced at an annual saving of $15,000. This showing pleased the viceroy, and he agreed to provide the $1000 needed for each new establishment on the condition that no added military force be called for. The guardian of San Fernando College was so notified August 19, 1796; and on September 29 he in turn announced to the viceroy that the required ten missionaries were ready, but begged that no reduction be made in the guards at the Missions already established. Lasuen felt that it would create large demands upon the old Missions to found so many new ones all at once, as they must help with cattle, horses, sheep, neophyte laborers, etc.; yet, to obtain the Missions, he was willing to do his very best, and felt sure his brave associates would further his efforts in every possible way. Thus it was that San José was founded, as before related, on June 11, 1797. The same day all returned to Santa Clara, and five days elapsed ere the guards and laborers were sent to begin work. Timbers were cut and water brought to the location, and soon the temporary buildings were ready for occupancy. By the end of the year there were 33 converts, and in 1800, 286. A wooden structure with a grass roof served as a church.

In 1809, April 23, the new church was completed, and Presidente Tapis came and blessed it. The following day he preached, and Padre Arroyo de la Cuesta said mass before a large congregation, including other priests, several of the military, and people from the pueblo and Santa Clara, and various neophytes. The following July the cemetery was blessed with the usual solemnities.

In 1811 Padre Fortuni accompanied Padre Abella on a journey of exploration to the Sacramento and San Joaquin valleys. They were gone fifteen days, found the Indians very timid, and thought the shores of the Sacramento offered a favorable site for a new Mission.

In 1817 Sergeant Soto, with one hundred San José neophytes, met twelve soldiers from San Francisco, and proceeded, by boat, to pursue some fugitives. They went up a river, possibly the San Joaquin, to a marshy island where, according to Soto's report, a thousand hostiles were assembled, who immediately fell upon their pursuers and fought them for three hours. So desperately did they fight, relying upon their superior numbers, that Soto was doubtful as to the result; but eventually they broke and fled, swimming to places of safety, leaving many dead and wounded but no captives. Only one neophyte warrior was killed.

In 1820 San José reported a population of 1754, with 6859 large stock, 859 horses, etc., and 12,000 sheep.

For twenty-seven years Padre Duran, who

from 1825 to 1827 was also the padre presidente, served Mission San José. In 1824 it reached its maximum of population in 1806 souls. In everything it was prosperous, standing fourth on the list both as to crops and herds.

Owing to its situation, being the first Mission reached by trappers, etc., from the east, and also being the nearest to the valleys of the Sacramento and San Joaquin, which afforded good retreats for fugitives, San José had an exciting history. In 1826 there was an expedition against the Cosumnes, in which forty Indians were killed, a ranchería destroyed, and forty captives taken. In 1829 the famous campaign against Estanislas, who has given his name to both a river and county, took place. This Indian was a neophyte of San José, and being of more than usual ability and smartness, was made alcalde. In 1827 or early in 1828 he ran away, and with a companion, Cipriano, and a large following, soon made himself the terror of the rancheros of the neighborhood. One expedition sent against him resulted disastrously, owing to insufficient equipment, so a determined effort under M. G. Vallejo, who was now the commander-in-chief of the whole California army, was made. May 29 he and his forces crossed the San Joaquin River on rafts, and arrived the next day at the scene of the former battle. With taunts, yells of defiance, and a shower of arrows, Estanislas met the coming army, he and his forces hidden in the fancied security of an impenetrable forest. Vallejo at once set men to work in different directions to fire the wood, which brought some of the Indians to the edge, where they were slain. As evening came on, twenty-five men and an officer entered the wood and fought until dusk, retiring with three men wounded. Next morning Vallejo, with thirty-seven soldiers, entered the wood, where he found pits, ditches, and barricades arranged with considerable skill. Nothing but fire could have dislodged the enemy. They had fled under cover of night. Vallejo set off in pursuit, and when, two days later, he surrounded them, they declared they would die rather than surrender. A road was cut through chaparral with axes, along which the field-piece and muskets were pressed forward and discharged. The Indians retreated slowly, wounding eight soldiers. When the cannon was close to the enemies' intrenchments the ammunition gave out, and this fact and the heat of the burning thicket compelled retreat. During the night the Indians endeavored to escape, one by one, but most of them were killed by the watchful guards. The next day nothing but the dead and three living women were found. There were some accusations, later, that Vallejo summarily executed some captives; but he denied it, and claimed that the only justification for any such charge arose from the fact that one man and one woman had been killed, the latter wrongfully by a soldier, whom he advised be punished.

Up to the time of secularization, the Mission continued to be one of the most prosperous. Jesus Vallejo was the administrator for secularization, and in 1837 he and Padre Gonzalez Rubio made an inventory which gave a total of over $155,000, when all debts were paid. Even now for awhile it seemed to prosper, and not until 1840 did the decline set in.

In accordance with Micheltorena's decree of March 29, 1843, San José was restored to the temporal control of the padres, who entered with good-will and zest into the labor of saving what they could out of the wreck. Under Pico's decree of 1845 the Mission was inventoried, but the document cannot nowbe found, nor a copy of it. The population was reported as 400 in 1842, and it is supposed that possibly 250 still lived at the Mission in 1845. On May 5, 1846, Pico sold all the property to Andrés Pico and J. B. Alvarado for $12,000, but the sale never went into effect.

Mission San José de Guadalupe and the pueblo of the same name are not, as so many people, even residents of California, think, one and the same. The pueblo of San José is now the modern city of that name, the home of the State Normal School, and the starting-point for Mount Hamilton. But Mission San José is a small settlement, nearly twenty miles east and north, in the foothills overlooking the southeast end of San Francisco Bay. The Mission church has entirely disappeared, an earthquake in 1868 having completed the ruin begun by the spoliation at the time of secularization. A modern parish church has since been built upon the site. Nothing of the original Mission now remains except a portion of the monastery. The corridor is without arches, and is plain and unpretentious, the roof being composed of willows tied to the roughly hewn log rafters with rawhide. Behind this is a beautiful old alameda of olives, at the upper end of which a modern orphanage, conducted by the Dominican Sisters, has been erected. This avenue of olives is crossed by another one at right angles, and both were planted by the padres in the early days, as is evidenced by the age of the trees. Doubtless many a procession of Indian neophytes has walked up and down here, even as I saw a procession of the orphans and their white-garbed guardians a short time ago. The surrounding garden is kept up in as good style under the care of the sisters as it was in early days by the padres.

The orphanage was erected in 1884 by Archbishop Alemany as a seminary for young men who wished to study for the priesthood, but it was never very successful in this work. For awhile it remained empty, then was offered to the Dominican Sisters as a boarding-school. But as this undertaking did not pay, in 1891 Archbishop Riordan offered such terms as led the Mother General of the Dominican Sisters to purchase it as an orphanage, and as such it is now most successfully conducted. There are at the present time about eighty children cared for by these sweet and gentle sisters of our Lord.

Two of the old Mission bells are hung in the new church. On one of these is the inscription: " S. S. José. Ano de 1826." And on the upper bell, " S. S. Joseph 1815, Ave María Purísima."

The old Mission baptismal font is also still in use. It is of hammered copper, about three feet in diameter, surmounted by an iron cross about eight inches high. The font stands upon a wooden base, painted, and is about four feet high.

CHAPTER XXIV

SAN JUAN BAUTISTA

THE second of the " filling up the links of the chain " Missions was that of San Juan Bautista. Three days after the commandant of San Francisco had received his orders to furnish a guard for the founders of Mission San José, the commandant of Monterey received a like order for a guard for the founders of San Juan Bautista. This consisted of five men and Corporal Ballesteros. By June 17 this industrious officer had erected a church, missionary-house, granary, and guard-house, and a week later Lasuen, with the aid of two priests, duly founded the new Mission. The site was a good one, and by 1800 crops to the extent of 2700 bushels were raised. At the same time 516 neophytes were reported — not bad for two and a half years' work.

In 1798 the gentiles from the mountains twenty-five miles east of San Juan, the Ansayames, surrounded the Mission by night, but were prevailed upon to retire. Later some of the neophytes ran away and joined these hostiles, and then a force was sent to capture the runaways and administer punishment. In the ensuing fight a chief was

FACHADA OF MISSION SAN JUAN BAUTISTA.

Photograph by Howard Tibbitts, San Francisco.
RUINED WALLS AND NEW BELL TOWER,
MISSION SAN JUAN BAUTISTA.

Photograph by Howard Tibbitts, San Francisco.
MISSION SAN JUAN BAUTISTA, FROM THE PLAZA.

Photograph by Howard Tibbitts, San Francisco.
THE ARCHED CORRIDOR, MISSION SAN JUAN BAUTISTA.

killed and another wounded, and two gentiles brought in to be forcibly educated. Other rancherías were visited, fifty fugitives arrested, and a few floggings and many warnings given.

This did not prevent the Ansayames, however, from killing two Mutsunes at San Benito Creek, burning a house and some wheat-fields, and seriously threatening the Mission. Moraga was sent against them and captured eighteen hostiles and the chiefs of the hostile rancherías.

Almost as bad as warlike Indians were the earthquakes of that year, several in number, which cracked all the adobe walls of the buildings and compelled everybody — friars and Indians — to sleep out of doors for safety.

In 1803 the governor ordered the padres of San Juan to remove their stock from La Brea rancho, which had been granted to Mariano Castro. They refused on the grounds that the rancho properly belonged to the Mission and should not have been granted to Castro, and on appeal the viceroy confirmed their contention.

In June of this year the corner-stone of a new church was laid. Padre Viader conducted the ceremonies, aided by the resident priests. Don José de la Guerra was the sponsor, and Captain Font and Surgeon Morelos assisted.

In June, 1809, the image of San Juan was placed on the high altar in the sacristy, which served for purposes of worship until the completion of the church.

By the end of the decade the population had grown to 702, though the number of deaths was large, and it continued slowly to increase until in 1823 it reached its greatest population with 1248 souls.

The new church was completed and dedicated on June 23, 1812. In 1818 a new altar was completed, and a painter named Chavez demanded six reals a day for decorating. As the Mission could not afford this, a Yankee, known as Felipe Santiago — properly Thomas Doak — undertook the work, aided by the neophytes. In 1815 one of the ministers was Estéban Tapis, who afterwards became the presidente.

In 1836 San Juan was the scene of the preparations for hostility begun by José Castro and Alvarado against Governor Gutierrez. Meetings were held at which excited speeches were made advocating revolutionary methods, and the fife and drum were soon heard by the peaceful inhabitants of the old Mission. Many of the whites joined in with Alvarado and Castro, and the affair ultimated in the forced exile of the governor; Castro took his place until Alvarado was elected by the *diputacion*.

The regular statistics of San Juan cease in 1832, when there were 916 Indians registered. In 1835, according to the decree of secularization, 63 Indians were " emancipated." Possibly these were the heads of families. Among these were to be distributed land valued at $5120, live-stock, including 41 horses, $1782, implements, effects, etc., $1467.

The summary of statistics from the founding of the Mission in 1797 to 1834 shows 4100 baptisms, 1028 marriages, 3027 deaths. The largest number of cattle owned was 11,000 in 1820, 1598 horses in 1806, 13,000 sheep in 1816.

In 1845, when Pico's decree was issued, San Juan was considered a pueblo, and orders given for the sale of all property except a curate's house, the church, and a court-house. The inventory gave a value of $8000. The population was now about 150, half of whom were whites and the other half Indians.

It will be remembered that it was at San Juan that Castro organized his forces to repel what he considered the invasion of Frémont in 1846. From Gavilan heights, near by, the explorer looked down and saw the warlike preparations directed against him, and from there wrote his declaration: " I am making myself as strong as possible, in the intention that if we are unjustly attacked we will fight to extremity and refuse quarter, trusting to our country to avenge our death."

In 1846 Pico sold all that remained of San Juan Bautista — the orchard — to O. Deleissèques for a debt, and though he did not obtain possession at the time, the United States courts finally confirmed his claim. This was the last act in the history of the once prosperous Mission.

The entrance at San Juan Bautista seems more

like that of a prison than a church. The Rev. Valentin Closa, of the Company of Jesus, who for many years has had charge here, found that some visitors were so irresponsible that thefts were of almost daily occurrence. So he had a wooden barrier placed across the church from wall to wall, and floor to ceiling, through which a gate affords entrance, and this gate is kept padlocked with as constant watchfulness as is that of a prison. Passing this barrier, the two objects that immediately catch one's eye are the semicircular arch dividing the church from the altar and the old wooden pulpit on the left.

Of the modern bell-tower it can only be said that it is a pity necessity seemed to compel the erection of such an abortion. The old padres seldom, if ever, failed in their architectural taste. However one may criticise their lesser work, such as the decorations, he is compelled to admire their *large* work; they were right, powerful, and dignified in their straightforward simplicity. And it is pathetic that in later days, when workmen and money were scarce, the modern priests did not see some way of overcoming obstacles that would have been more harmonious with the old plans than is evidenced by this tower and many other similar incongruities, such as the steel bell-tower at San Miguel.

At San Juan Bautista the old reredos remains, though the altar is new. The six figures of the saints are the original ones placed there when it was

Photograph by Howard Tibbitts, San Francisco.

STAIRWAY LEADING TO PULPIT, MISSION SAN JUAN BAUTISTA.

Photograph by Howard Tibbitts, San Francisco.

DOORWAY, MISSION SAN JUAN BAUTISTA.

MISSION SAN MIGUEL ARCANGEL, FROM THE SOUTH.

MISSION SAN MIGUEL ARCANGEL AND CORRIDORS.

first erected. In the center, at the top, is Our Lady of Guadalupe; to the left, San Antonio de Padua; to the right, San Isadore de Madrid (the patron saint of all farmers); below, in the center, is the saint of the Mission, San Juan Bautista, on his left, St. Francis, and on his right, San Buenaventura.

The baptistery is on the left, at the entrance. Over its old, solid, heavy doors rises a half-circular arch. Inside are two bowls of heavy sandstone.

In the belfry are two bells, one of which is modern, cast in San Francisco. The other is the largest Mission bell, I believe, in California. It bears the inscription: " Ave María Purísima S. Fernando RVELAS me Fecit 1809."

There is a small collection of objects of interest connected with the old Mission preserved in one room of the monastery. Among other things are two of the chorals; pieces of rawhide used for tying the beams, etc., in the original construction; the head of a bass-viol that used to be played by one of the Indians; a small mortar; and quite a number of books. Perhaps the strangest thing in the whole collection is an old barrel-organ made by Benjamin Dobson, The Minories, London. It has several barrels and on one of them is the following list of its tunes: Go to the Devil; Spanish Waltz; College Hornpipe; Lady Campbell's Reel. One can imagine with what feelings one of the sainted padres, after a peculiarly trying

day with his aboriginal children, would put in
this barrel, and while his lips said holy things, his
hand instinctively ground out with vigor the first
piece on the list.

CHAPTER XXV

SAN MIGUEL, ARCÁNGEL

LASUEN's third Mission, of 1797, was San Miguel, located near a large ranchería named *Sagshpileel*, and on the site called *Vahiá*. One reason for the selection of the location is given in the fact that there was plenty of water at Santa Isabel and San Marcos for the irrigation of three hundred fanegas of seed. To this day the springs of Santa Isabel are a joy and delight to all who know them, and the remains of the old irrigating canals and dams, dug and built by the padres, are still to be seen.

On the day of the founding, Lasuen's heart was made glad by the presentation of fifteen children for baptism. At the end of 1800 there were 362 neophytes, 372 horses and cattle, and 1582 smaller animals. The crop of 1800 was 1900 bushels.

Padre Antonio de la Concepción Horra, who was shortly after deported as insane, and who gave Presidente Lasuen considerable trouble by preferring serious charges against the Missions, was one of the first ministers.

In February of 1801 the two padres were attacked with violent pains in the stomach and they feared the neophytes had poisoned them, but they soon recovered. Padre Pujol, who came from Monterey to aid them, did not fare so well, for he was taken sick in a similar manner and died. Three Indians were arrested, but it was never decided whether poison had been used or not. The Indians escaped when being taken north to the presidio, and eventually the padres pleaded for their release, asking however that they be flogged in the presence of their families for having boasted that they had poisoned the padres.

In August, 1806, a disastrous fire occurred, destroying all the manufacturing part of the establishment as well as a large quantity of wool, hides, cloth, and 6000 bushels of wheat. The roof of the church was also partially burned. At the end of the decade San Miguel had a population of 973, and in the number of its sheep it was excelled only by San Juan Capistrano.

In 1818 a new church was reported as ready for roofing, and this was possibly built to replace the one partially destroyed by fire in 1806. In 1814 the Mission registered its largest population in 1076 neophytes, and in live-stock it showed satisfactory increase at the end of the decade, though in agriculture it had not been so successful.

Ten years later it had to report a great diminution in its flocks and herds and its neophytes. The soil and pasture were also found to be poor, though vines flourished and timber was plentiful. Robinson, who visited San Miguel at this time, reports it as a poor establishment and tells a large story about the heat suffocating the fleas. Padre Martin died in 1824.

In 1834 there were but 599 neophytes on the register. In 846 Ignacio Coronel took charge in order to carry out the order of secularization, and when the inventory was made it showed the existence of property, excluding everything pertaining to the church, of $82,000. In 1839 this amount was reduced to $75,000. This large valuation was owing to the fact that there were several ranches and buildings and two large vineyards belonging to the Mission. These latter were Santa Isabel and Aguage, with 5500 vines, valued at $22,162.

The general statistics from the founding in 1797 to 1834 give 2588 baptisms, 2038 deaths; largest population was 1076 in 1814. The largest number of cattle was 10,558 in 1822, horses 1560 in 1822, mules 140 in 1817, sheep 14,000 in 1820.

In 1836 Padre Moreno reported that when Coronel came all the available property was distributed among the Indians, except the grain, and of that they carried off more than half. In 1838 the poor padre complained bitterly of his poverty and the disappearance of the Mission property. There is no doubt but that here as elsewhere the Mission was plundered on every hand, and the officers appointed to guard its interests were among the plunderers.

In 1844 Presidente Duran reported that San

Miguel had neither lands nor cattle, and that i·s neophytes were demoralized and scattered for want of a minister. Pico's 1845 decree warned the Indians that they must return within a month and occupy their lands, or they would be disposed of; and in 1846 Pico reported the Mission sold, though no consideration is named, to P. Rios and Wm. Reed. The purchasers took possession, but the courts later declared their title invalid. In 1848 Reed and his whole family were atrociously murdered. The murderers were pursued; one was fatally wounded, one jumped into the sea and was drowned, and the other three were caught and executed.

The register of baptisms at San Miguel begins July 25, 1797, and up to 1861 contains 2917 names. Between the years 1844 and 1851 there is a vacancy, and only one name occurs in the latter year. The title-page is signed by Fr. Fermin Franco de Lasuen, and the priests in charge are named as Fr. Buenaventura Sitjar and Fr. Antonio de la Concepción.

At the end of this book is a list of 43 children of the " gentes de razon " included in the general list, but here specialized for reference.

The registry of deaths contains 2249 names up to 1841. The first entry is signed by Fr. Juan Martin and the next two by Fr. Sitjar.

The old marriage register of the Mission of San Miguel is now at San Luis Obispo. It has a title-page signed by Fr. Lasuen.

In 1888 some of the old bells of the Mission were sent to San Francisco and there were recast into one large bell, weighing 2500 pounds. Until 1902 this stood on a rude wooden tower in front of the church, but in that year an incongruous steel tower took its place. Packed away in a box still remains one of the old bells, which has sounded its last call. A large hole is in one side of it. The inscription, as near as I can make out, reads "A. D. 1800, S. S. Gabriel."

In 1901 the outside of the church and monastery was restored with a coat of new plaster and cement. Inside nearly everything is as it was left by the robber hand of secularization.

On the walls are the ten oil paintings brought by the original founders. They are very indistinct in the dim light of the church, and little can be said of their artistic value without further examination.

There is also an old breviary with two heavy, hand-made clasps, dated Antwerp, 1735, and containing the autograph of Fr. Man. de Castañeda.

There is a quadrangle at San Miguel 230 feet square, and on one side of it a corridor corresponding to the one in front, for six pillars of burnt brick still remain.

At the rear of the church was the original church, used before the present one was built, and a number of remains of the old houses of the neophytes still stand, though in a very dilapidated condition.

San Miguel was always noted for its proximity

to the Hot Springs and Sulphur Mud Baths of
Paso Robles.   Both Indians and Mission padres
knew of their healthful and curative properties, and
in the early days scores of thousands enjoyed their
peculiar virtues.   Little by little the " superior
race " is learning that in natural therapeutics
the Indian is a reasonably safe guide to follow;
hence the present extensive use by the whites of
the Mud and Sulphur Baths at Paso Robles.
Methinks the Indians of a century ago, though
doubtless astonished at the wonderful temple to
the white man's God built at San Miguel, would
wonder much more were they now to see the
elaborate and splendid house recently erected at
Paso Robles for the purpose of giving to more
white people the baths, the virtue of which
they so well knew.

SEEKING TO PREVENT THE PHOTOGRAPHER FROM MAKING A PICTURE OF
MISSION SAN MIGUEL ARCANGEL.

OLD PULPIT AT MISSION SAN MIGUEL ARCANGEL.

RESTORED MONASTERY AND MISSION CHURCH OF SAN FERNANDO REY.

CORRIDORS AT SAN FERNANDO REY.

CHAPTER XXVI

SAN FERNANDO, REY DE ESPAGNA

On September 8, 1797, the seventeenth of the California Missions was founded by Padre Lasuen, in the Encino Valley, where Francisco Reyes had a rancho in the Los Angeles jurisdiction. The natives called it *Achois Comihavit*. Reyes' house was appropriated as a temporary dwelling for the missionary. The Mission was dedicated to Fernando III, King of Spain. Lasuen came down from San Miguel to Santa Barbara, especially for the foundation, and from thence with Sergeant Olivera and a military escort. These, with Padre Francisco Dumetz, the priest chosen to have charge, and his assistant, Francisco Favier Uría, composed, with the large concourse of Indians, the witnesses of the solemn ceremonial.

On the fourth of October Olivera reported the guard-house and storehouse finished, two houses begun, and preparations already being made for the church.

From the baptismal register it is seen that ten children were baptized the first day, and thirteen adults were received early in October. By the end of 1797 there were fifty-five neophytes.

Three years after its founding 310 Indians were gathered in, and its year's crop was 1000 bushels of grain. The Missions of San Juan Capistrano, San Gabriel, San Buenaventura, and Santa Barbara had contributed live-stock, and now its herds had grown to 526 horses, mules, and cattle, and 600 sheep.

In December, 1806, an adobe church, with a tile roof, was consecrated, which on the 21st of December, 1812, was severely injured by the earthquake that did damage to almost all the Missions of the chain. Thirty new beams were needed to support the injured walls. A new chapel was built, which was completed in 1818.

In 1834 Lieutenant Antonio del Valle was the comisionado appointed to secularize the Mission, and the next year he became majordomo and served until 1837.

It was on his journey north, in 1842, to take hold of the governorship, that Micheltorena learned at San Fernando of Commodore Jones's raising of the American flag at Monterey. By his decree, also, in 1843, San Fernando was ordered returned to the control of the padres, which was done, though the next year Duran reported that there were but few cattle left, and two vineyards.

Micheltorena was destined again to appear at San Fernando, for when the Californians under Pio Pico and Castro rose to drive out the Mexicans, the governor finally capitulated at the same place, as he had heard the bad news of the Americans' capture of Monterey. February 21, 1845, after a bloodless " battle " at Cahuenga, he " abdicated," and finally left the country and returned to Mexico.

In 1845 Juan Manso and Andrés Pico leased the Mission at a rental of $1120, the affairs having been fairly well administered by Padre Orday after its return to the control of the friars. A year later it was sold by Pio Pico, under the order of the assembly, for $14,000, to Eulogio Célis, whose title was afterwards confirmed by the courts. Orday remained as pastor until May, 1847, and was San Fernando's last minister under the Franciscans.

In 1847 San Fernando again heard the alarm of war. Frémont and his battalion reached here in January, and remained until the signing of the treaty of Cahuenga, which closed all serious hostilities against the United States in its conquest of California.

Connected with the Mission of San Fernando is the first discovery of California gold. Eight years before the great days of '49 Francisco Lopez, the *mayordomo* of the Mission, was in the canyon of San Feliciano, which is about eight miles westerly from the present town of Newhall, and according to Don Abel Stearns, " with a companion, while in search of some stray horses, about midday stopped under some trees and tied their horses to feed. While resting in the shade, Lopez with his sheath knife dug up some wild onions, and in the dirt discovered a piece of gold. Searching further, he found more. On his return to town he showed these pieces to his friends, who at once declared there must be a placer of gold there."

Then the rush began. As soon as the people in Los Angeles and Santa Barbara heard of it, they flocked to the new " gold fields " in hundreds. And the first California gold dust ever coined at the government mint at Philadelphia came from these mines. It was taken around Cape Horn in a sailing-vessel by Alfred Robinson, the translator of Boscana's *Indians of California*, and consisted of 18.34 ounces, and made $344.75, or over $19 to the ounce.

Davis says that in the first two years after the discovery not less than from $80,000 to $100,000 was gathered. Don Antonio Coronel, with three Indian laborers, in 1842, took out $600 worth of dust in two months.

Water being scarce, the methods of washing the gravel were both crude and wasteful. And it is interesting to note that the first gold " pans " were *bateas*, or bowl-shaped Indian baskets.

The church at San Fernando is in a completely ruined condition. It stands southwest to northeast. The entrance is at the southwest end and the altar at the northeast. There is also a side entrance at the east, with a half-circular arch, sloping into a larger arch inside, with a flat top and rounded upper corners. The thickness of

Photograph by Harold A. Parker, Pasadena.
SHEEP AT MISSION SAN FERNANDO REY.

RUINS OF OLD ADOBE WALL AND CHURCH, MISSION SAN FERNANDO REY.

Photograph by George Wharton James.

MONASTERY AND OLD FOUNTAIN AT MISSION SAN FERNANDO REY.

Photograph by C.C. Pierce & Co., Los Angeles.

INTERIOR OF RUINED CHURCH, MISSION SAN FERNANDO REY.

the walls allows the working out of various styles in these outer and inner arches that is curious and interesting. They reveal the individuality of the builder, and as they are all structural and pleasing, they afford a wonderful example of variety in adapting the arch to its necessary functions.

The graveyard is on the northwest side of the church, and close by is the old olive orchard, where a number of fine trees are still growing. There are also two large palms, pictures of which are generally taken with the Mission in the background, and the mountains beyond. It is an exquisite subject. The remains of adobe walls still surround the orchard.

The doorway leading to the graveyard is of a half-circle inside, and slopes outward, where the arch is square.

There is a buttress of burnt brick to the southeast of the church, which appears as if it might have been an addition after the earthquake.

At the monastery the chief entrance is a simple but effective arched doorway, now plastered and whitewashed. The double door frame projects pilaster-like, with a four-membered cornice above, from which rises an elliptical arch, with an elliptical cornice about a foot above.

From this monastery one looks out upon a court or plaza which is literally dotted with ruins, though they are mainly of surrounding walls. Immediately in the foreground is a fountain, the reservoir of which is built of brick covered with cement.   A double bowl rests on the center standard.

Further away in the court are the remnants of what may have been another fountain, the reservoir of which is made of brick, built into a singular geometrical figure. This is composed of eight semicircles, with V's connecting them, the apex of each V being on the outside. It appears like an attempt at creating a conventionalized flower in brick.

Two hundred yards or so away from the monastery is a square structure, the outside of boulders. Curiosity prompting, you climb up, and on looking in you find that inside this framework of boulders are two circular cisterns of brick, fully six feet in diameter across the top, decreasing in size to the bottom, which is perhaps four feet in diameter.

In March, 1905, considerable excitement was caused by the actions of the parish priest of San Fernando, a Frenchman named Le Bellegny, of venerable appearance and gentle manners. Not being acquainted with the *status quo* of the old Mission, he exhumed the bodies of the Franciscan friars who had been buried in the church and reburied them. He removed the baptismal font to his church, and unroofed some of the old buildings and took the tiles and timbers away. As soon as he understood the matter he ceased his operations, but, unfortunately, not before considerable damage was done.

CHAPTER XXVII

SAN LUIS, REY DE FRANCIA

THE last Mission of the century, the last of Lasuen's administration, and the last south of Santa Barbara, was that of San Luis Rey. Lasuen himself explored the region and determined the site. The governor agreed to it, and on February 27, 1798, ordered a guard to be furnished from San Diego who should obey Lasuen implicitly and help erect the necessary buildings for the new Mission. The founding took place on June 13, in the presence of Captain Grajera and his guard, a few San Juan neophytes, and many gentiles, Presidente Lasuen performing the ceremonies, aided by Padres Peyri and Santiago. Fifty-four children were baptized at the same time, and from the very start the Mission was prosperous. No other missionary has left such a record as Padre Peyri. He was zealous, sensible, and energetic. He knew what he wanted and how to secure it. The Indians worked willingly for him, and by the 1st of July six thousand adobes were made for the church. By the end of 1800 there were 237 neophytes, 617 larger stock, and 1600 sheep.

The new church was completed in 1801–1802, but Peyri was too energetic to stop at this. Buildings of all kinds were erected, and neophytes gathered in so that by 1810 its population was 1519, with the smallest death rate of any Mission. In 1811 Peyri petitioned the governor to allow him to build a new and better church of adobes and bricks; but as consent was not forthcoming, he went out to Pala, and in 1816 established a branch establishment, built a church, and the picturesque campanile now known all over the world, and soon had a thousand converts tilling the soil and attending the services of the church.

In 1826 San Luis Rey reached its maximum in population with 2869 neophytes. From now on began its decline, though in material prosperity it was far ahead of any other Mission. In 1828 it had 28,900 sheep, and the cattle were also rapidly increasing. The average crop of grain was 12,660 bushels.

San Luis Rey was one of the Missions where a large number of cattle were slaughtered on account of the secularization decree. It is said that some 20,000 head were killed at the San Jacinto Rancho alone. The Indians were much stirred up over the granting of the ranchos, which they claimed were their own lands. Indeed they formed a plot to capture the governor on one of his southern trips in order to protest to him against the granting of the Temécula Rancho.

The final secularization took place in November,

Photograph by Howard Tibbitts, San Francisco.

HOUSE OF MEXICAN, MADE FROM RUINED WALL AND TILES OF MISSION
SAN FERNANDO REY.

Photograph by Harold A. Parker, Pasadena.

THE RUINED ALTAR, MORTUARY CHAPEL, SAN LUIS REY.

ILLUMINATED CHOIR MISSALS, ETC., AT MISSION SAN LUIS REY.

1834, with Captain Portilla as comisionado and Pio Pico as majordomo and administrator until 1840. There was trouble in apportioning the lands among the Indians, for Portilla called for fifteen or twenty men to aid him in quelling disturbances; and at Pala the majordomo was knocked down and left for dead by an Indian. The inventory showed property (including the church, valued at $30,000) worth $203,707, with debts of $93,000. The six ranchos were included as worth $40,437, the three most valuable being Pala, Santa Margarita, and San Jacinto.

Micheltorena's decree of 1843 restored San Luis Rey to priestly control, but by that time its spoliation was nearly complete. Padre Zalvidea was in his dotage, and the four hundred Indians had scarcely anything left to them. Two years later the majordomo, appointed by Zalvidea to act for him, turned over the property to his successor, and the inventory shows the frightful wreckage. Of all the vast herds and flocks, only 279 horses, 20 mules, 61 asses, 196 cattle, 27 yoke oxen, 700 sheep, and a few valueless implements remained. All the ranchos had passed into private ownership.

May 18, 1846, all that remained of the former king of Missions was sold by Pio Pico to Cot and José Pico for $2437. Frémont dispossessed their agent and they failed to gain repossession, the courts deciding that Pico had no right to sell. In 1847 the celebrated Mormon battalion, which

Parkman so vividly describes in his *Oregon Trail*, were stationed at San Luis Rey for two months, and later on, a re-enlisted company was sent to take charge of it for a short time. On their departure Captain Hunter, as sub-Indian agent, took charge and found a large number of Indians, amenable to discipline and good workers.

The general statistics from the founding in 1798 to 1834 show 5591 baptisms, 1425 marriages, 2859 deaths. In 1832 there were 27,500 cattle, 2226 horses in 1828, 345 mules in the same year, 28,913 sheep in 1828, and 1300 goats in 1832.

In 1892 Father J. J. O'Keefe, who had done excellent work at Santa Barbara, was sent to San Luis Rey to repair the church and make it suitable for a missionary college of the Franciscan Order. May 12, 1893, the rededication ceremonies of the restored building took place, the bishop of the diocese, the vicar-general of the Franciscan Order and other dignitaries being present and aiding in the solemnities. Three old Indian women were also there who heard the mass said at the original dedication of the church in 1802. Since that time Father O'Keefe has raised and expended thousands of dollars in repairing, always keeping in mind the original plans. He also rebuilt the monastery.

San Luis Rey is now a college for the training of missionaries for the field, and its work is in charge of Father Peter Wallischeck, who was for so many years identified with the College of the Franciscans at Santa Barbara.

Immediately on entering the church one observes doorways to the right and left — the one on the right bricked up. It is the door that used to lead to the stairway of the bell-tower. In 1913 the doorway was opened. The whole tower was found to be filled with adobe earth, why, no one really knows, though it is supposed it may have been to preserve the structure from falling in case of an earthquake.

A semicircular arch spans the whole church from side to side, about thirty feet, on which the original decorations still remain. These are in rude imitation of marble, as at Santa Barbara, in black and red, with bluish green lines. The wall colorings below are in imitation of black marble.

The choir gallery is over the main entrance, and there a great revolving music-stand is still in use, with several of the large and interesting illuminated manuscript singing-books of the early days. In Mission days it was generally the custom to have two chanters, who took care of the singing and the books. These, with all the other singers, stood around the revolving music-stand, on which the large manuscript chorals were placed.

The old Byzantine pulpit still occupies its original position at San Luis Rey, but the sounding-board is gone — no one knows whither. This is of a type commonly found in Continental churches, the corbel with its conical sides harmonizing with the ten panels and base-mouldings of the box proper. It is fastened to the pilaster which supports the arch above.

The original paint — a little of it — still remains. It appears to have been white on the panels, lined in red and blue.

The pulpit was entered from the side altar, through a doorway pierced through the wall. The steps leading up to it are of red burnt brick. Evidently it was a home product, and was possibly made by one of Padre Peyri's Indian carpenters, who was rapidly nearing graduation into the ranks of the skilled cabinet-makers.

The Mortuary Chapel is perhaps as fine a piece of work as any in the whole Mission chain. It is beautiful even now in its sad dilapidation. It was crowned with a domed roof of heavy cement. The entrance was by the door in the church to the right of the main entrance. The room is octagonal, with the altar in a recess, over which is a dome of brick, with a small lantern. At each point of the octagon there is an engaged column, built of circular-fronted brick which run to a point at the rear and are thus built into the wall. A three-membered cornice crowns each column, which supports arches that reach from one column to another. There are two windows, one to the southeast, the other northwest. The altar is at the northeast. There are two doorways, with stairways which lead to a small outlook over the altar and the whole interior. These

Photograph by Fred W. Twogood, Riverside.

GRAVEYARD, RUINS OF MORTUARY CHAPEL AND TOWER, MISSION SAN LUIS REY.

Photograph by Howard Tibbitts, San Francisco.

BELFRY WINDOW, MISSION SAN FERNANDO REY.

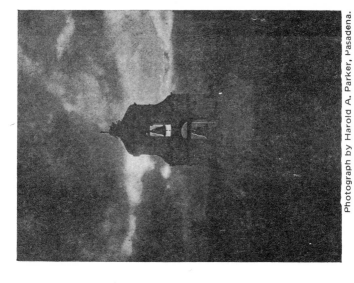

Photograph by Harold A. Parker, Pasadena.

THE CAMPANILE AT PALA.

Copyright, 1900, by G.P. Thresher.

SIDE OF MISSION SAN LUIS REY.

were for the watchers of the dead, so that at a glance they might see that nothing was disturbed.

The altar and its recess are most interesting, the rear wall of the former being decorated in classic design.

This chapel is of the third order of St. Francis, the founder of the Franciscan Order. In the oval space over the arch which spans the entrance to the altar are the " arms " of the third order, consisting of the Cross and the five wounds (the stigmata) of Christ, which were conferred upon St. Francis as a special sign of divine favor.

Father Wallischeck is now (1913) arranging for the complete restoration of this beautiful little chapel and appeals for funds to aid in the work.

CHAPTER XXVIII

" BEAUTIFUL for situation " was the spot selected for the only Mission founded during the
first decade of the nineteenth century, — Santa
Inés.

Governor Borica, who called California " the
most peaceful and quiet country on earth," and
under whose orders Padre Lasuen had established
the five Missions of 1796–1797, had himself made
explorations in the scenic mountainous regions of
the coast, and recommended the location afterwards determined upon, called by the Indians
Alajulapu, meaning *rincon*, or corner.

The native population was reported to number
over a thousand, and the fact that they were
frequently engaged in petty hostilities among
themselves rendered it necessary to employ unusual care in initiating the new enterprise. Presidente Tapis therefore asked the governor for a
larger guard than was generally assigned for
protecting the Missions, and a sergeant and nine
men were ordered for that purpose.

The distance from Santa Barbara was about
thirty-five miles, over a rough road, hardly more

than a trail, winding in and out among the foothills, and gradually climbing up into the mountains in the midst of most charming and romantic
scenery. The quaint procession, consisting of
Padre Presidente Tapis and three other priests,
Commandant Carrillo, and the soldiers, and a
large number of neophytes from Santa Barbara,
slowly marched over this mountainous road, into
the woody recesses where nestled the future home
of the Mission of Santa Inés, and where the
usual ceremonies of foundation took place September 17, 1804. Padres Calzada, Gutierrez,
and Ciprès assisted Presidente Tapis, and the two
former remained as the missionaries in charge.

The first result of the founding of this Mission
was the immediate baptism of twenty-seven
children, a scene worthy of the canvas of a genius,
could any modern painter conceive of the real
picture, — the group of dusky little ones with
somber, wondering eyes, and the long-gowned
priests, with the soldiers on guard and the watchful Indians in native costume in the background,
— all in the temple of nature's creating.

The first church erected was not elaborate, but
it was roofed with tiles, and was ample in size
for all needful purposes. In 1812 an earthquake
caused a partial collapse of this structure. The
corner of the church fell, roofs were ruined, walls
cracked, and many buildings near the Mission
were destroyed. This was a serious calamity,
but the padres never seemed daunted by adverse

circumstances. They held the usual services in a granary, temporarily, and in 1817 completed the building of a new church constructed of brick and adobe, which still remains. In 1829 the Mission property was said to resemble that at Santa Barbara. On one side were gardens and orchards, on the other houses and Indian huts, and in front was a large enclosure, built of brick and used for bathing and washing purposes.

When Governor Chico came up to assume his office in 1835 he claimed to have been insulted by a poor reception from Padre Jimeno at Santa Inés. The padre said he had had no notice of the governor's coming, and therefore did the best he could. But Presidente Duran took the bold position of informing the governor, in reply to a query, that the government had no claim whatever upon the hospitality of unsecularized Missions. Chico reported the whole matter to the assembly, who sided with the governor, rebuked the presidente and the padres, and confirmed an order issued for the immediate secularization of Santa Inés and San Buenaventura (Duran's own Mission). J. M. Ramirez was appointed comisionado at Santa Inés. At this time the Mission was prosperous. The inventory showed property valued at $46,186, besides the church and its equipment. The general statistics from the foundation, 1804 to 1834, show 1372 baptisms, 409 marriages, and 1271 deaths. The largest number of cattle was 7300 in 1831, 800 horses in 1816, and 6000 sheep in 1821. After secularization horses were taken for the troops, and while, for a time, the cattle increased, it was not long before decline set in.

In 1843 the management of the Mission was restored to the friars, but the former conditions of prosperity had passed away never to return. Two years later the estate was rented for $580 per year, and was finally sold in 1846 for $1700, although in later times the title was declared invalid. In the meantime an ecclesiastical college was opened at Santa Inés in 1844. A grant of land had been obtained from the government, and an assignment of $500 per year to the seminary on the condition that no Californian in search of a higher education should ever be excluded from its doors; but the project met with only a temporary success, and was abandoned after a brief existence of six years.

In 1844 Presidente Duran reported 264 neophytes at Santa Inés, with sufficient resources for their support. When Pico's order of 1845 was issued, the Mission was valued at $20,288. This did not include the church, the curate's house or rooms, and the rooms needed for the court-house. This inventory was taken without the co-operation of the padre, who refused to sign it. He — the padre — remained in charge until 1850, when the Mission was most probably abandoned.

At Santa Inés there were several workers in leather and silver whose reputation still remains. In various parts of the State are specimens of the saddles they made and carved and then inlaid in silver that are worthy a place in any noteworthy collection of artistic work.

Only ten arches remain at Santa Inés of the long line of corridor arches that once graced this building. In the distance is a pillar of one still standing alone. Between it and the last of the ten, eight others used to be, and beyond it there are the clear traces of three or four more.

The church floor is of red tiles. All the window arches are plain semicircles. Plain, rounded, heavy mouldings about three feet from the floor, and the same distance from the ceiling, extend around the inside of the church, making a simple and effective structural ornament.

The original altar is not now used. It is hidden behind the more pretentious modern one. It is of cement, or plastered adobe, built out, like a huge statue bracket, from the rear wall. The old tabernacle, ornate and florid, is still in use, though showing its century of service. There are also several interesting candlesticks, two of which are pictured in the chapter on woodwork.

Almost opposite the church entrance is a large reservoir, built of brick, twenty-one feet long and eight feet wide. It is at the bottom of a walled-in pit, with a sloping entrance to the reservoir proper, walls and slope being of burnt brick. This " sunk enclosure " is about sixty feet long and thirty feet across at the lower end, and about six feet below the level to the edge of the reservoir.

MISSION SANTA INES.

MISSION SAN RAFAEL ARCANGEL.

From an old painting.

MISSION SAN FRANCISCO SOLANO, AT SONOMA.

Connected with this by a cement pipe or tunnel laid underground, over 660 feet long, is another reservoir over forty feet long, and eight feet wide, and nearly six feet deep. This was the reservoir which supplied the Indian village with water. The upper reservoir was for the use of the padres and also for bathing purposes.

The water supply was brought from the mountains several miles distant, flumed where necessary, and then conveyed underground in cement pipes made and laid by the Indians under the direction of the padres. The water-right is now lost to the Mission, being owned by private parties.

The earthquake of 1906 caused considerable damage at Santa Inés, and it has not yet been completely repaired, funds for the purpose not having been forthcoming.

CHAPTER XXIX

SAN RAFAEL, ARCÁNGEL

THE Mission of the Archangel, San Rafael, was founded to give a health resort to a number of neophytes who were sick in San Francisco. The native name for the site was *Nanaguani*. The date of founding was December 14, 1817. There were about 140 neophytes transferred at first, and by the end of 1820 the number had increased to 590. In 1818 a composite building, including church, priest's house, and all the apartments required, was erected. It was of adobe, 87 feet long, 42 feet wide, and 18 feet high, and had a corridor of tules. In 1818, when Presidente Payeras visited the Mission, he was not very pleased with the site, and after making a somewhat careful survey of the country around recommended several other sites as preferable.

In 1824 a determined effort was made to capture a renegade neophyte of San Francisco, a native of the San Rafael region, named Pomponio, who for several years had terrorized the country at intervals as far south as Santa Cruz. He would rob, outrage, and murder, confining most of his attacks, however, upon the Indians. He had

slain one soldier, Manuel Varela, and therefore
a determined effort was made for his capture.
Lieutenant Martinez, a corporal, and two men
found him in the Canyada de Novato, above
San Rafael. He was sent to Monterey, tried by
a court-martial on the 6th of February, and
finally shot the following September. This same
Martinez also had some conflicts about the same
time with chieftains of hostile tribes, north of the
bay, named Marin and Quentin, both of whom
have left names, one to a county and the other
to a point on the bay.

When San Francisco Solano was founded, 92
neophytes were sent there from San Rafael.
In spite of this, the population of San Rafael increased until it numbered 1140 in 1828.

In 1824 Kotzebue visited the Mission and spoke
enthusiastically of its natural advantages, though
he made but brief reference to its improvements.
On his way to Sonoma, Duhaut-Cilly did not deem
it of sufficient importance to more than mention.
Yet it was a position of great importance. Governor Echeandía became alarmed about the activity of the Russians at Fort Ross, and accused
them of bad faith, claiming that they enticed
neophytes away from San Rafael, etc. The
Mexican government, in replying to his fears,
urged the foundation of a fort, but nothing was
done, owing to the political complications at the
time, which made no man's tenure of office certain.

The secularization decree ordered that San Rafael should become a parish of the first class, which class paid its curates $1500, as against $1000 to those of the second class.

In 1837 it was reported that the Indians were not using their liberty well; so, owing to the political troubles at the time, General Vallejo was authorized to collect everything and care for it under a promise to redistribute when conditions were better. In 1840 the Indians insisted upon this promise being kept, and in spite of the governor's opposition Vallejo succeeded in obtaining an order for the distribution of the live-stock.

In 1845 Pico's order, demanding the return within one month of the Indians to the lands of San Rafael or they would be sold, was published, and the inventory taken thereupon showed a value of $17,000 in buildings, lands, and live-stock. In 1846 the sale was made to Antonio Suñol and A. M. Pico for $8000. The purchasers did not obtain possession, and their title was afterwards declared invalid.

In the distribution of the Mission stock Vallejo reserved a small band of horses for the purposes of national defense, and it was this band that was seized by the " Bear Flag " revolutionists at the opening of hostilities between the Americans and Mexicans. This act was followed almost immediately by the joining of the insurgents by Frémont, and the latter's marching to meet the

Mexican forces, which were supposed to be at San Rafael. No force, however, was found there, so Frémont took possession of the Mission on June 26, 1846, and remained there for about a week, leaving there to chase up Torre, who had gone to join Castro. When he finally left the region he took with him a number of cattle and horses, went to Sonoma, and on the 5th of July assumed active command of all the insurgent forces, which ultimated in the conquest of the State.

From this time the ex-Mission had no history. The buildings doubtless suffered much from Frémont's occupancy, and never being very elaborate, easily fell a prey to the elements.

There is not a remnant of them now left, and the site is occupied by a modern, hideous, wooden building, used as an armory.

CHAPTER XXX

SAN FRANCISCO SOLANO

FIFTY-FOUR years after the founding of the first Franciscan Mission in California, the site was chosen for the twenty-first and last, San Francisco Solano. This Mission was established at Sonoma under conditions already narrated. The first ceremonies took place July 4, 1823, and nine months later the Mission church was dedicated. This structure was built of boards, but by the end of 1824 a large building had been completed, made of adobe with tiled roof and corridor, also a granary and eight houses for the use of the padres and soldiers. Thus in a year and a half from the time the location was selected the necessary Mission buildings had been erected, and a large number of fruit trees and vines were already growing. The neophytes numbered 693, but many of these were sent from San Francisco, San José and San Rafael. The Indians at this Mission represented thirty-five different tribes, according to the record, yet they worked together harmoniously, and in 1830 their possessions included more than 8000 cattle, sheep, and horses. Their crops averaged nearly 2000 bushels of grain per year.

The number of baptisms recorded during the twelve years before secularization was over 1300. Ten years later only about 200 Indians were left in that vicinity.

In 1834 the Mission was secularized by M. G. Vallejo, who appointed Ortega as majordomo. Vallejo quarreled with Padre Quijas, who at once left and went to reside at San Rafael. The movable property was distributed to the Indians, and they were allowed to live on their old rancherías, though there is no record that they were formally allotted to them. By and by the gentile Indians so harassed the Mission Indians that the latter placed all their stock under the charge of General Vallejo, asking him to care for it on their behalf. The herds increased under his control, the Indians had implicit confidence in him, and he seems to have acted fairly and honestly by them.

The pueblo of Sonoma was organized as a part of the secularization of San Francisco Solano, and also to afford homes for the colonists brought to the country by Hijar and Padrés. In this same year the soldiers of the presidio of San Francisco de Asis were transferred to Sonoma, to act as a protection of the frontier, to overawe the Russians, and check the incoming of Americans. This meant the virtual abandonment of the post by the shores of the bay. Vallejo supported the presidial company, mainly at his own expense, and made friends with the native chief, Solano, who aided him materially in keeping the Indians peaceful.

The general statistics of the Mission for the eleven years of its existence, 1823–34, are as follows: baptisms 1315, marriages 278, deaths 651. The largest population was 996 in 1832. The largest number of cattle was 4849 in 1833, 1148 horses and 7114 sheep in the same year.

In 1845, when Pico's plan for selling and renting the Missions was formulated, Solano was declared without value, the secularization having been completely carried out, although there is an imperfect inventory of buildings, utensils, and church property. It was ignored in the final order. Of the capture of Sonoma by the Bear Flag revolutionists and the operations of Frémont, it is impossible here to treat. They are to be found in every good history of California.

In 1880 Bishop Alemany sold the Mission and grounds of San Francisco Solano to a German named Schocken for $3000. With that money a modern church was erected for the parish, which is still being used. For six months after the sale divine services were still held in the old Mission, and then Schocken used it as a place for storing wine and hay. In September, 1903, it was sold to the Hon. W. R. Hearst for $5000. The ground plot was 166 by 150 feet. It is said that the tower was built by General Vallejo in 1835 or thereabouts. The deeds have been transferred to the State of California and accepted by the Legislature. The intention is to preserve the Mission as a valuable historic landmark.

CHAPTER XXXI

THE MISSION CHAPELS OR ASISTENCIAS

THE Mission padres were the first circuit riders or pastors. It is generally supposed that the circuit rider is a device of the Methodist church, but history clearly reveals that long prior to the time of the sainted Wesley, and the denomination he founded, the padres were " riding the circuit," or walking, visiting the various rancherías which had no settled pastor.

Where buildings for worship were erected at these places they were called chapels, or asistencias. Some of these chapels still remain in use and the ruins of others are to be seen. The Mission of San Gabriel had four such chapels, viz., Los Angeles, Puente, San Antonio de Santa Ana, and San Bernardino. Of the first and the last we have considerable history.

LOS ANGELES CHAPEL

As I have elsewhere shown, it was the plan of the Spanish Crown not only to Christianize and civilize the Indians of California, but also to colonize the country. In accordance with this plan the pueblo of San José was founded on the

29th of November, 1776. The second was that of Los Angeles in 1781. Rivera was sent to secure colonists in Sonora and Sinaloa for the new pueblo, and also for the establishments it was intended to found on the channel of Santa Barbara.

In due time colonists were secured, and a more mongrel lot it would be hard to conceive: Indian, Spanish, Negro, Indian and Spanish, and Indian and Negro bloods were represented, 42 souls in all. The blood which makes the better Spanish classes in Los Angeles to-day so proud represents those who came in much later.

There was nothing accidental in the founding of any Spanish colony. Everything was planned beforehand. The colonist obeyed orders as rigidly executed as if they were military commands. According to Professor Guinn:

"The area of a pueblo, under Spanish rule, was four square leagues, or about 17,770 acres. The pueblo lands were divided into *solares* (house lots), *suertes*[1] (fields for planting), *dehesas* (outside pasture lands), *ejidos* (commons), *propios* (lands rented or leased), *realengas* (royal lands)."

On the arrival of the colonists in San Gabriel from Loreto on the 18th of August, 1781, Governor Neve issued instructions for founding Los Angeles

---

[1] *Suerte.* This is colloquial. It really means "chance" or "haphazard." In other words, it was the piece of ground that fell to the settler by "lot."

on the 26th. The first requirement was to select a site for a dam, to provide water for domestic and irrigation purposes. Then to locate the plaza and the homes and fields of the colonists. Says Professor Guinn:

" The old plaza was a parallelogram 100 varas [1] in length by 75 in breadth. It was laid out with its corners facing the cardinal points of the compass, and with its streets running at right angles to each of its four sides, so that no street would be swept by the wind. Two streets, each 10 varas wide, opened out on the longer sides, and three on each of the shorter sides. Upon three sides of the plaza were the house lots, 20 by 40 varas each, fronting on the square. One-half the remaining side was reserved for a guard-house, a town-house, and a public granary. Around the embryo town, a few years later, was built an adobe wall — not so much, perhaps, for protection from foreign invasion as from domestic intrusion. It was easier to wall in the town than to fence the cattle and goats that pastured outside."

The government supplied each colonist with a pair each of oxen, mules, mares, sheep, goats, and cows, one calf, a burro, a horse, and the branding-irons which distinguished his animals from those of the other settlers. There were also certain tools furnished for the colony as a whole.

On the 14th of September of the same year the plaza was solemnly dedicated. A father from the

[1] A vara is the Spanish yard of 33 inches.

San Gabriel Mission recited mass, a procession circled the plaza, bearing the cross, the standard of Spain, and an image of "Our Lady," after which salvos of musketry were fired and general rejoicings indulged in. Of course the plaza was blessed, and we are even told that Governor Neve made a speech.

As to when the first church was built in Los Angeles there seems to be some doubt. In 1811 authority was gained for the erection of a new chapel, but nowhere is there any account of a prior building. Doubtless some temporary structure had been used. There was no regular priest settled here, for in 1810 the citizens complained that the San Gabriel padres did not pay enough attention to their sick. In August of 1814 the corner-stone of the new chapel was laid by Padre Gil of San Gabriel, but nothing more than laying the foundation was done for four years. Then Governor Sola ordered that a higher site be chosen. The citizens subscribed five hundred cattle towards the fund, and Prefect Payeras made an appeal to the various friars which resulted in donations of seven barrels of brandy, worth $575. With these funds the work was done, José Antonio Ramirez being the architect, and his workers neophytes from San Gabriel and San Luis Rey, who were paid a real (twelve and a half cents) per day. Before 1821 the walls were raised to the window arches. The citizens, however, showed so little interest in the matter that it was not until Payeras made another appeal to his friars that *they* contributed enough to complete the work. Governor Sola gave a little, and the citizens a trifle. It is interesting to note what the contributions of the friars were. San Miguel offered 500 cattle, San Luis Obispo 200 cattle, Santa Barbara a barrel of brandy, San Diego two barrels of white wine, Purísima six mules and 200 cattle, San Fernando one barrel brandy, San Gabriel two barrels brandy, San Buenaventura said it would try to make up deficits or supply church furniture, etc. Thus Payeras's zeal and the willingness of the Los Angeleños to pay for wine and brandy, which they doubtless drank " to the success of the church," completed the structure, and December 8, 1822, it was formally dedicated. Auguste Wey writes:

"The oldest church in Los Angeles is known in local American parlance as ' The Plaza Church,' ' Our Lady,' ' Our Lady of Angels,' ' Church of Our Lady,' ' Church of the Angels,' ' Father Liébana's Church,' and ' The Adobe Church.' It is formally the church of Nuestra Señora, Reina de los Angeles — Our Lady, Queen of the Angels — from whom Los Angeles gets its name."

That is, the city gets its name from Our Lady, the Queen of the Angels, not from the church, as the pueblo was named long before the church was even suggested.

The plaza was formally moved to its present

site in 1835, May 23, when the government was changed from that of a pueblo to a city.

Concerning the name of the pueblo and river, Rev. Joachin Adam, vicar general of the diocese, in a paper read before the Historical Society of Southern California several years ago, said:

" The name Los Angeles is probably derived from the fact that the expedition by land, in search of the harbor of Monterey, passed through this place on the 2d of August, 1769, a day when the Franciscan missionaries celebrate the feast of Nuestra Señora de los Angeles — Our Lady of the Angels. This expedition left San Diego July 14, 1769, and reached here on the first of August, when they killed for the first time some *berrendos*, or antelope. On the second, they saw a large stream with much good land, which they called Porciúncula on account of commencing on that day the jubilee called Porciúncula, granted to St. Francis while praying in the little church of Our Lady of the Angels, near Assisi, in Italy, commonly called Della Porciúncula from a hamlet of that name near by. This was the original name of the Los Angeles River."

The last two recorded burials within the walls of the Los Angeles chapel are those of the young wife of Nathaniel M. Pryor, " buried on the left-hand side facing the altar," and of Doña Eustaquia, mother of the Dons Andrés, Jesus, and Pio Pico, all intimately connected with the history of the later days of Mexican rule.

CHAPEL OF SAN BERNARDINO

It must not be forgotten that one of the early methods of reaching California was inland. Travelers came from Mexico, by way of Sonora, then crossed the Colorado River and reached San Gabriel and Monterey in the north, over practically the same route as that followed to-day by the Southern Pacific Railway, viz., crossing the river at Yuma, over the Colorado Desert, by way of the San Gorgonio Pass, and through the San Bernardino and San Gabriel valleys. It was in 1774 that Captain Juan Bautista de Anza, of the presidio of Tubac in Arizona, was detailed by the Viceroy of New Spain to open this road. He made quite an expedition of it, — 240 men, women, and Indian scouts, and 1050 animals. They named the San Gorgonio Pass the Puerto de San Carlos, and the San Bernardino Valley the Valle de San José. Cucamonga they called the Arroyo de los Osos (Bear Ravine or Gulch).

As this road became frequented San Gabriel was the first stopping-place where supplies could be obtained after crossing the desert. This was soon found to be too far away, and for years it was desired that a station nearer to the desert be established, but not until 1810 was the decisive step taken. Then Padre Dumetz of San Gabriel, with a band of soldiers and Indian neophytes, set out, early in May, to find a location and establish such a station. They found a populous Indian ranchería, in a region well watered and luxuriant, and which bore a name significant of its desirability. The valley was *Guachama*, " the place of abundance of food and water," and the Indians had the same name. A station was established near the place now known as Bunker Hill, between Urbita Springs and Colton, and a " capilla," built, dedicated to San Bernardino, because it was on May 20, San Bernardino's feast-day, that Padre Dumetz entered the valley. The trustworthiness of the Indians will be understood when it is recalled that this chapel, station, and the large quantity of supplies were left in their charge, under the command of one of their number named Hipolito. Soon the station became known, after this Indian, as Politana.

The destruction of Politana in 1810 by savage and hostile Indians, aided by earthquakes, was a source of great distress to the padres at San Gabriel, and they longed to rebuild. But the success of the attack of the unconverted Indians had reawakened the never long dormant predatory instincts of the desert Indians, and, for several years, these made frequent incursions into the valley, killing not only the whites, but such Indians as seemed to prefer the new faith to the old. But in 1819 the Guachamas sent a delegation to San Gabriel, requesting the padres to come again, rebuild the Mission chapel, and re-establish the supply station, and giving assurances of protection and good behavior. The padres gladly acceded to the requests made, and in 1820 solemn chants and earnest exhortations again resounded in the ears of the Guachamas in a new and larger building of adobe erected some eight miles from Politana.

There are a few ruined walls still standing of the chapel of San Bernardino at this time, and had it not been for the care recently bestowed upon them, there would soon have been no remnant of this once prosperous and useful asistencia of the Mission of San Gabriel.

CHAPEL OF SAN MIGUEL

In 1803 a chapel was built at a ranchería called by the Indians *Mescaltitlan*, and the Spaniards San Miguel, six miles from Santa Barbara. It was of adobes, twenty-seven by sixty-six feet. In 1807 eighteen adobe dwellings were erected at the same place.

CHAPEL OF SAN MIGUELITO

One of the vistas of San Luis Obispo was a ranchería known as San Miguelito, and here in 1809 the governor gave his approval that a chapel should be erected. San Luis had several such vistas, and I am told that the ruins of several chapels are still in existence in that region.

CHAPEL AT SANTA ISABEL (SAN DIEGO)

In 1816–19 the padres at San Diego urged the governor to give them permission to erect a chapel at Santa Isabel, some forty miles away, where two hundred baptized Indians were living. The governor did not approve, however, and nothing was done until after 1820. By 1822 the chapel was reported built, with several houses, a granary, and a graveyard. The population had increased to 450, and these materially aided San Diego in keeping the mountainous tribes, who were hostile, in check.

A recent article in a Southern California magazine thus describes the ruins of the Mission of Santa Isabel:

" Levelled by time, and washed by winter rains, the adobe walls of the church have sunk into indistinguishable heaps of earth which vaguely define the outlines of the ancient edifice. The bells remain, hung no longer in a belfry, but on a rude framework of logs. A tall cross, made of two saplings nailed in shape, marks the consecrated spot. Beyond it rise the walls of the brush building, *enramada*, woven of green wattled boughs, which does duty for a church on Sundays and on the rare occasions of a visit from the priest, who makes a yearly pilgrimage to these outlying portions of his diocese. On Sundays, the Captain of the tribe acts as lay reader and recites the services. Then and on Saturday nights the bells are rung. An Indian boy has the office of bell-ringer, and crossing the ropes attached to the clappers, he skilfully makes a solemn chime."

The graveyard at Santa Isabel is neglected and forlorn, and yet bears many evidences of the loving thoughtfulness of the loved ones who remain behind.

CHAPEL OF MESA GRANDE

Eleven miles or so from Santa Isabel, up a steep road, is the Indian village of Mesa Grande. The ranchería (as the old Spaniards would call it) occupies a narrow valley and sweep of barren hillside. On a level space at the foot of the mountain the little church is built. Santo Domingo is the patron saint.

A recent visitor thus describes it:

" The church was built like that of Santa Isabel, of green boughs, and the chancel was decorated with muslin draperies and ornaments of paper and ribbon, in whose preparation a faithful Indian woman had spent the greater part of five days. The altar was furnished with drawn-work cloths, and in a niche above it was a plaster image of Santo Domingo, one hand holding a book, the other outstretched in benediction. Upon the outstretched hand a rosary had been hung with appropriate effect. Some mystic letters appeared in the muslin that draped the ceiling, which, being interpreted, proved to be the initials of the solitary member of the altar guild, and of such of her family as she was pleased to commemorate."

CHAPEL OF SANTA MARGARITA (SAN LUIS OBISPO)

One of the ranchos of San Luis Obispo was that of Santa Margarita on the north side of the Sierra Santa Lucia. As far as I know there is no record of the date when the chapel was built, yet it was a most interesting and important structure.

In May, 1904, its identity was completely destroyed, its interior walls being dynamited and removed and the whole structure roofed over to be used as a barn.

It originally consisted of a chapel about 40 feet long and 30 feet wide, and eight rooms. The chapel was at the southwest end. The whole building was 120 feet long and 20 feet wide. The walls were about three feet thick, and built of large pieces of rough sandstone and red bricks, all cemented strongly together with a white cement that is still hard and tenacious. It is possible there was no *fachada* to the chapel at the southwest end, for a well-built elliptical arched doorway, on the southeast side, most probably was the main entrance.

It has long been believed that this was not the only Mission building at Santa Margarita. Near by are three old adobe houses, all recently renovated out of all resemblance to their original condition, and all roofed with red Mission tiles. These were built in the early days. The oldest Mexican inhabitants of the present-day Santa Margarita remember them as a part of the Mission building.

Here, then, is explanation enough for the assumption of a large Indian population on this ranch, which led the neighboring padres to establish a chapel for their Christianization and civilization. Undoubtedly in its aboriginal days there was a large Indian population, for there were all the essentials in abundance. Game of every kind — deer, antelope, rabbits, squirrels, bear, ducks, geese, doves, and quail — yet abound; also roots of every edible kind, and more acorns than in any other equal area in the State. There is a never failing flow of mountain water and innumerable springs, as well as a climate at once warm and yet bracing, for here on the northern slopes of the Santa Lucia, frost is not uncommon.

CHAPEL OF SANTA ISABEL (SAN MIGUEL)

I have elsewhere referred to the water supply of Santa Isabel as being used for irrigation connected with San Miguel Mission. There is every evidence that a large ranchería existed at Santa Isabel, and that for many years it was one of the valued rancheros of the Mission. Below the Hot Springs the remains of a large dam still exist, which we now know was built by the padres for irrigation purposes. A large tract of land below was watered by it, and we have a number of reports of the annual yield of grain, showing great fertility and productivity. Near the present ranch house at Santa Isabel are large adobe ruins, evidently used as a house for the majordomo and for the padre on his regular visitations to the ranchería. One of the larger rooms was doubtless a chapel where mass was said for the neophytes who cultivated the soil in this region.

CHAPEL OF SAN ANTONIO DE PALA

The chapel at Pala is perhaps the best known of all the asistencias on account of its picturesque campanile. It was built by the indefatigable Padre Peyri, in 1816, and is about twenty miles from San Luis Rey, to which it belonged. Within a year or two, by means of a resident padre, over a thousand converts were gathered, reciting their prayers and tilling the soil. A few buildings, beside the chapel, were erected, and the community, far removed from all political strife, must have been happy and contented in its mountain-valley home. The chapel is a long, narrow adobe structure, 144 by 27 feet, roofed with red tiles. The walls within were decorated in the primitive and singular fashion found at others of the Missions, and upon the altar were several statues which the Indians valued highly.

Pala is made peculiarly interesting as the present home of the evicted Palatingwa (Hot Springs) Indians of Warner's Ranch. Here these wretchedly treated " wards of the nation " are now struggling with the problem of life, with the fact ever before them, when they think, (as they often do, for several of them called my attention to the fact) that the former Indian population of Pala has totally disappeared. At the time of the secularization of San Luis Rey, Pala suffered with the rest; and when the Americans finally took possession it was abandoned to the tender

MAIN DOORWAY AT SANTA MARGARITA CHAPEL.

ANOTHER VIEW OF THE CAMPANILE AND CHAPEL, SAN ANTONIO
DE PALA.

CAMPANILE AND CHAPEL, SAN ANTONIO DE PALA.

mercies of the straying, seeking, searching, devouring homesteader. In due time it was " homesteaded." The chapel and graveyard were ultimately deeded back; and when the Landmarks Club took hold it was agreed that the ruins " revert to their proper ownership, the church."

Though all the original Indians were ousted long ago from their lands at Pala, those who lived anywhere within a dozen or a score miles still took great interest in the old buildings, the decorations of the church, and the statues of the saints. Whenever a priest came and held services a goodly congregation assembled, for a number of Mexicans, as well as Indians, live in the neighborhood.

That they loved the dear old asistencia was manifested by Americans, Mexicans, and Indians alike, for when the Landmarks Club visited it in December, 1901, and asked for assistance to put it in order, help was immediately volunteered to the extent of $217, if the work were paid for at the rate of $1.75 per day.

With a desire to promote the good feeling aimed at in recent dealings with the evicted Indians of Warner's Ranch, now located at Pala, the bishop of the diocese sent them a priest. He, however, was of an alien race, and unfamiliar with either the history of the chapel, its memories, or the feelings of the Indians; and to their intense indignation, they found that without consulting them, or his own superiors, he had destroyed nearly all the interior decorations by covering them with a coating of whitewash.

The building now is in fairly good condition and the Indians have a pastor who holds regular services for them. In the main they express themselves as highly contented with their present condition, and on a visit paid them in April, 1913, I found them happy and prosperous.

CHAPTER XXXII

THE PRESENT CONDITION OF THE MISSION INDIANS

THE disastrous effect of the order of secularization upon the Indians, as well as the Missions themselves, has been referred to in a special chapter. Here I wish to give, in brief, a clearer idea of the present condition of the Indians than was there possible. In the years 1833–1837 secularization actually was accomplished. The knowledge that it was coming had already done much injury. The Pious Fund, which then amounted to upwards of a half-million dollars, was confiscated by the Mexican government. The officials said it was merely " borrowed." This practically left the Indians to their own resources. A certain amount of land and stock were to be given to each head of a family, and tools were to be provided. Owing to the long distance between California and the City of Mexico, there was much confusion as to how the changes should be brought about. There have been many charges made, alleging that the padres wilfully allowed the Mission property to go to ruin, when they were deprived of its control. This ruin would better be attributed to the general demoralization of the times than to any definite policy. For it must be remembered that the political conditions of Mexico at that time were most unsettled. None knew what a day or an hour might bring forth. All was confusion, uncertainty, irresponsibility. And in the *mêlée* Mission property and Mission Indians suffered.

What was to become of the Indians? Imagine the father of a family — that had no mother — suddenly snatched away, and all the property, garden, granary, mill, storehouse, orchards, cattle, placed in other hands. What would the children do?

So now the Indians, like bereft children, knew not what to do, and, naturally, they did what our own children would do. Led by want and hunger, some sought and found work and food, and others, alas, became thieves. The Mission establishment was the organized institution that had cared for them, and had provided the work that supported them. No longer able to go and live " wildly " as of old, they were driven to evil methods by necessity unless the new government directed their energies into right channels. Few attempted to do this; hence the results that were foreseen by the padres followed.

July 7, 1846, saw the Mexican flag in California hauled down, and the Stars and Stripes raised in its place; but as far as the Indian was concerned, the change was for the worse instead of the better.

Indeed, it may truthfully be said that the policies of the three governments, Spanish, Mexican, and American, have shown three distinct phases, and that the last is by far the worst.

Our treatment of these Indians reads like a hideous nightmare. Absolutely no forceful and effective protest seems to have been made against the indescribable wrongs perpetrated. The gold discoveries of 1849 brought into the country a class of adventurers, gamblers, liquor sellers, and camp followers of the vilest description. The Indians became helpless victims in the hands of these infamous wretches, and even the authorities aided to make these Indians " good."

Bartlett, who visited the country in 1850 to 1853, tells of meeting with an old Indian at San Luis Rey who spoke glowingly of the good times they had when the padres were there, but " now," he said, " they were scattered about, he knew not where, without a home or protectors, and were in a miserable, starving condition." Of the San Francisco Indians he says:

" They are a miserable, squalid-looking set, squatting or lying about the corners of the streets, without occupation. They have now no means of obtaining a living, as their lands are all taken from them; and the Missions for which they labored, and which provided after a sort for many thousands of them, are abolished. No care seems to be taken of them by the Americans; on the contrary, the effort seems to be to exterminate them as soon as possible."

According to the most conservative estimates there were over thirty thousand Indians under the control of the Missions at the time of secularization in 1833. To-day, how many are there? I have spent long days in the different Mission localities, arduously searching for Indians, but oftentimes only to fail of my purpose. In and about San Francisco, there is not one to be found. At San Carlos Borromeo, in both Monterey and the Carmelo Valley, except for a few half-breeds, no one of Indian blood can be discovered. It is the same at San Miguel, San Luis Obispo, and Santa Barbara. At Pala, that romantic chapel, where once the visiting priest from San Luis Rey found a congregation of several hundreds awaiting his ministrations, the land was recently purchased from white men, by the United States Indian Commission, as a new home for the evicted Palatingwa Indians of Warner's Ranch. These latter Indians, in recent interviews with me, have pertinently asked: "Where did the white men get this land, so they could sell it to the government for us? Indians lived here many centuries before a white man had ever seen the 'land of the sun-down sea.' When the 'long-gowns' first came here, there were many Indians at Pala. Now they are all gone. Where? And how do we know that before long we shall not be driven out, and be gone, as they were driven out and are gone?"

At San Luis Rey and San Diego, there are a few scattered families, but very few, and most of these have fled far back into the desert, or to the high mountains, as far as possible out of reach of the civilization that demoralizes and exterminates them.

A few scattered remnants are all that remain.

Let us seek for the real reason why.

The system of the padres was patriarchal, paternal. Certain it is that the Indians were largely treated as if they were children. No one questions or denies this statement. Few question that the Indians were happy under this system, and all will concede that they made wonderful progress in the so-called arts of civilization. From crude savagery they were lifted by the training of the fathers into usefulness and productiveness. They retained their health, vigor, and virility. They were, by necessity perhaps, but still undeniably, chaste, virtuous, temperate, honest, and reasonably truthful. They were good fathers and mothers, obedient sons and daughters, amenable to authority, and respectful to the counsels of old age.

All this and more may unreservedly be said for the Indians while they were under the control of the fathers. That there were occasionally individual cases of harsh treatment is possible. The most loving and indulgent parents are now and again ill-tempered, fretful, or nervous. The fathers were men subject to all the limitations of other men. Granting these limitations and making due allowance for human imperfection, the rule of the fathers must still be admired for its wisdom and commended for its immediate results.

Now comes the order of secularization, and a little later the domination of the Americans. Those opposed to the control of the fathers are to set the Indians free. They are to be " removed from under the irksome restraint of cold-blooded priests who have held them in bondage not far removed from slavery " ! ! They are to have unrestrained liberty, the broadest and fullest intercourse with the great American people, the white, Caucasian American, not the dark-skinned Mexican! ! !

What was the result. Let an eye-witness testify:

" These thousands of Indians had been held in the most rigid discipline by the Mission Fathers, and after their emancipation by the Supreme Government of Mexico, had been reasonably well governed by the local authorities, who found in them indispensable auxiliaries as farmers and harvesters, hewers of wood and drawers of water, and besides, the best horse-breakers and herders in the world, necessary to the management of the great herds of the country. These Indians were Christians, docile even to servility, and excellent laborers. Then came the Americans, followed soon after by the discovery of, and the wild rush for, gold, and the relaxation for the time being of a healthy administration of the laws. The ruin of this once happy and useful people commenced. The cultivators of vineyards began to pay their Indian *peons* with *aguardiente*, a

real ' firewater.' The consequence was that on receiving their wages on Saturday evening, the laborers
habitually met in great gatherings and passed the night
in gambling, drunkenness, and debauchery. On Sunday
the streets were crowded from morning until night with
Indians, — males and females of all ages, from the
girl of ten or twelve to the old man and woman of
seventy or eighty.

" By four o'clock on Sunday afternoon, Los Angeles
Street, from Commercial to Nigger Alley, Aliso Street
from Los Angeles to Alameda, and Nigger Alley, were
crowded with a mass of drunken Indians, yelling and
fighting: men and women, boys and girls using tooth
and nail, and frequently knives, but always in a manner
to strike the spectator with horror.

" At sundown, the pompous marshal, with his
Indian special deputies, who had been confined in jail
all day to keep them sober, would drive and drag the
combatants to a great corral in the rear of the Downey
Block, where they slept away their intoxication. The
following morning they would be exposed for sale, as
slaves for the week. Los Angeles had its slave-mart
as well as New Orleans and Constantinople, — only the
slaves at Los Angeles were sold fifty-two times a year, as
long as they lived, a period which did not generally
exceed one, two, or three years under the new dispen-
sation. They were sold for a week, and bought up by
vineyard men and others at prices ranging from one to
three dollars, one-third of which was to be paid to the
peon at the end of the week, which debt, due for well-
performed labor, was invariably paid in *aguardiente*,
and the Indian made happy, until the following Monday
morning, he having passed through another Saturday

night and Sunday's saturnalia of debauchery and bestiality. Those thousands of honest, useful people were absolutely destroyed in this way."

In reference to these statements of the sale of the Indians as slaves, it should be noted that the act was done under the cover of the law. The Indian was " fined " a certain sum for his drunkenness, and was then turned over to the tender mercies of the employer, who paid the fine. Thus " justice " was perverted to the vile ends of the conscienceless scoundrels who posed as " officers of the law."

Charles Warren Stoddard, one of California's sweetest poets, realized to the full the mercenary treatment the Missions and the Indians had received, and one of the latest and also most powerful poems he ever wrote, "The Bells of San Gabriel," deals with this spoliation as a theme. The poem first appeared in *Sunset Magazine, the Pacific Monthly*, and with the kind consent of the editor I give the last stanza.

" Where are they now, O tower!
    The locusts and wild honey?
Where is the sacred dower
    That the Bride of Christ was given?
Gone to the wielders of power,
    The misers and minters of money;
Gone for the greed that is their creed —
    And these in the land have thriven.
What then wert thou, and what art now,
    And wherefore hast thou striven?

REFRAIN

And every note of every bell
Sang Gabriel! rang Gabriel!
In the tower that is left the tale to tell
Of Gabriel, the Archangel."

To-day, the total Indian population of Southern California is reported as between two and three thousand. It is not increasing, and it is good for the race that it is not. Until the incumbency by W. A. Jones of the Indian Commissionership in Washington, there seems to have been little or no attempt at effective protection of the Indians against the land and other thefts of the whites. The facts are succinctly and powerfully stated by Helen Hunt Jackson in her report to the government, and in her *Glimpses of California and the Missions*. The indictment of churches, citizens, and the general government, for their crime of supineness in allowing our acknowledged wards to be seduced, cheated, and corrupted, should be read by every honest American; even though it make his blood seethe with indignation and his nerves quiver with shame.

In my larger work on this subject I published a table from the report of the agent for the " Mission-Tule " Consolidated Agency, which is dated September 25, 1903.

This is the official report of an agent whom not even his best friends acknowledge as being over-fond of his Indian charges, or likely to be sentimental in his dealings with them. , What does this report state? Of twenty-eight " reservations " — and some of these include several Indian villages — it announces that the lands of eight are yet " not patented." In other words, that the Indians are living upon them " on sufferance." Therefore, if any citizen of the United States, possessed of sufficient political power, so desired, the lands could be restored to the public domain. Then, not even the United States Supreme Court could hold them for the future use and benefit of the Indians.

On five of these reservations the land is " desert," and in two cases, " subject to intense heat " (it might be said, to 150 degrees, and even higher in the middle of summer); in one case there is " little water for irrigation."

In four cases it is " poor land," with " no water," and in another instance there are " worthless, dry hills; " in still another the soil is " almost worthless for lack of water! "

In one of the desert cases, where there are five villages, the government has supplied " water in abundance for irrigation and domestic use, from artesian wells." Yet the land is not patented, and the Indians are helpless, if evicted by resolute men.

At Cahuilla, with a population of one hundred fifty-five, the report says, " mountain valley; stock land and little water. Not patented."

At Santa Isabel, including Volcan, with a

population of two hundred eighty-four, the reservation of twenty-nine thousand eight hundred forty-four acres is patented, but the report says it is " mountainous; stock land; no water."

At San Jacinto, with a population of one hundred forty-three, the two thousand nine hundred sixty acres are " mostly poor; very little water, and not patented."

San Manuel, with thirty-eight persons, has a patent for six hundred forty acres of " worthless, dry hills."

Temecula, with one hundred eighty-one persons, has had allotted to its members three thousand three hundred sixty acres, which area, however, is " almost worthless for lack of water."

Let us reflect upon these things! The poor Indian is exiled and expelled from the lands of his ancestors to worthless hills, sandy desert, grazing lands, mostly poor and mountainous land, while our powerful government stands by and professes its helplessness to prevent the evil. These discouraging facts are enough to make the just and good men who once guided the republic rise from their graves. Is there a remnant of honor, justice, or integrity, left among our politicians?

There is one thing this government should have done, could have done, and might have done, and it is to its discredit and disgrace that it did not do it; that is, when the treaty of Guadalupe Hidalgo transferred the Indians from the domination of

Mexico to that of the United States, this government " of, for, and by " the people, should have recognized the helplessness of its wards and not passed a law of which they could not by any possibility know, requiring them to file on their lands, but it should have appointed a competent guardian of their moral and legal rights, taking it for granted that *occupancy of the lands of their forefathers would give them a legal title which would hold forever against all comers.*

In all the Spanish occupation of California it is doubtful whether one case ever occurred where an Indian was driven off his land.

In rendering a decision on the Warner's Ranch Case the United States Supreme Court had an opportunity offered it, once for all to settle the status of all American Indians. Had it familiarized itself with the laws of Spain, under which all Spanish grants were made, it would have found that the Indian was always considered first and foremost in all grants of lands made. He must be protected in his right; it was inalienable. He was helpless, and therefore the officers of the Crown were made responsible for his protection. If subordinate officers failed, then the more urgent the duty of superior officers. Therefore, even had a grant been made of Warner's Ranch in which the grantor purposely left out the recognition of the rights of the Indians, the highest Spanish courts would not have tolerated any such abuse of power. This was an axiom of Spanish rule, shown by a hundred, a thousand precedents. Hence it should have been recognized by the United States Supreme Court. It is good law, but better, it is good sense and common justice, and this is especially good when it protects the helpless and weak from the powerful and strong.

In our dealings with the Indians in our school system, we are making the mistake of being in too great a hurry. A race of aborigines is not raised into civilization in a night. It will be well if it is done in two or three generations.

Contrast our method with that followed by the padres. Is there any comparison? Yes! To our shame and disgrace. The padres kept fathers and mothers and children together, at least to a reasonable degree. Where there were families they lived — as a rule — in their own homes near the Missions. Thus there was no division of families. On the other hand, we have wilfully and deliberately, though perhaps without *malice aforethought* (although the effect has been exactly the same as if we had had malice), separated children from their parents and sent them a hundred, several hundred, often two or three *thousand* miles away from home, there to receive an education often entirely inappropriate and incompetent to meet their needs. And even this sending has not always been honorably done. *Vide* the United States Indian Commissioner's report for 1900. He says:

" These pupils are gathered from the cabin, the wickiup, and the tepee. *Partly by cajolery and partly by threats; partly by bribery and partly by fraud; partly by persuasion and partly by force,* they are induced to leave their homes and their kindred to enter these schools and take upon themselves the outward semblance of civilized life. They are chosen not on account of any particular merit of their own, not by reason of mental fitness, but solely because they have Indian blood in their veins.   Without regard to their worldly condition; without any previous training; without any preparation whatever, they are transported to the schools — sometimes thousands of miles away — without the slightest expense or trouble to themselves or their people.

" The Indian youth finds himself at once, as if by magic, translated from a state of poverty to one of affluence. He is well fed and clothed and lodged. Books and all the accessories of learning are given him and teachers provided to instruct him. He is educated in the industrial arts on the one hand, and not only in the rudiments but in the liberal arts on the other. Beyond the three r's he is instructed in geography, grammar, and history; he is taught drawing, algebra and geometry, music and astronomy and receives lessons in physiology, botany, and entomology. Matrons wait on him while he is well, and physicians and nurses attend him when he is sick. A steam laundry does his washing, and the latest modern appliances do his cooking. A library affords him relaxation for his leisure hours, athletic sports and the gymnasium furnish him exercise and recreation, while music entertains him in the evening. He has hot and cold baths, and steam heat and electric light, and all the modern conveniences. All the necessities of life are given him, and many of the luxuries. All of this without money and without price, or the contribution of a single effort of his own or of his people. His wants are all supplied almost for the wish. The child of the wigwam becomes a modern Aladdin, who has only to rub the government lamp to gratify his desires.

"Here he remains until his education is finished, when he is returned to his home — which by contrast must seem squalid indeed — to the parents whom his education must make it difficult to honor, and left to make his way against the ignorance and bigotry of his tribe. Is it any wonder he fails? Is it surprising if he lapses into barbarism? Not having earned his education, it is not appreciated; having made no sacrifice to obtain it, it is not valued. It is looked upon as a right and not as a privilege; it is accepted as a favor to the government and not to the recipient, and the almost inevitable tendency is to encourage dependency, foster pride, and create a spirit of arrogance and selfishness. The testimony on this point of those closely connected with the Indian employees of the service would, it is believe, be interesting."

So there the matter stands. Nothing of any great importance was really done to help the Indians except the conferences at Mohonk, N. Y., until, in 1902, the Sequoya League was organized, composed of many men and women of national prominence, with the avowed purpose " to make better Indians." In its first pronunciamento it declared:

"The first struggle will be not to arouse sympathy but to inform with slow patience and long wisdom the wide-spread sympathy which already exists. We cannot take the Indians out of the hands of the National Government; we cannot take the National Government into our own hands. Therefore we must work with the National Government in any large plan for the betterment of Indian conditions.

"The League means, in absolute good faith, not to fight, but to assist the Indian Bureau. It means to give the money of many and the time and brains and experience of more than a few to honest assistance to the Bureau in doing the work for which it has never had either enough money or enough disinterested and expert assistance to do in the best way the thing it and every American would like to see done."

CHAPTER XXXIII

MISSION ARCHITECTURE

THE question is often asked: Is there a Mission architecture? It is not my intention here to discuss this question *in extenso,* but merely to answer it by asking another and then making an affirmation. What is it that constitutes a style in architecture? It cannot be that every separate style must show different and distinct features from every other style. It is not enough that in each style there are specific features that, when combined, form an appropriate and harmonious relationship that distinguishes it from every other combination.

As a rule, the Missions were built in the form of a hollow square: the church representing the *fachada,* with the priests' quarters and the houses for the Indians forming the wings. These quarters were generally colonnaded or cloistered, with a series of semicircular arches, and roofed with red tiles. In the interior was the *patio* or court, which often contained a fountain and a garden. Upon this *patio* opened all the apartments: those of the fathers and of the majordomo, and the guest-rooms, as well as the workshops, schoolrooms and storehouses.

One of the strongest features of this style, and one that has had a wide influence upon our modern architecture, is the stepped and curved sides of the pediment.

This is found at San Luis Rey, San Gabriel, San Antonio de Padua, Santa Inés, and at other places. At San Luis Rey, it is the dominant feature of the extension wall to the right of the *fachada* of the main building.

On this San Luis pediment occurs a lantern which architects regard as misplaced. Yet the fathers' motive for its presence is clear: that is, the uplifting of the Sign whereby the Indians could alone find salvation.

Another means of uplifting the cross was found in the domes — practically all of which were terraced — on the summits of which the lantern and cross were placed.

The careful observer may note another distinctive feature which was seldom absent from the Mission domes. This is the series of steps at each " corner " of the half-dome. Several eminent architects have told me that the purpose of these steps is unknown, but to my simple lay mind it is evident that they were placed there purposely by the clerical architects to afford easy access to the surmounting cross; so that any accident to this sacred symbol could be speedily remedied. It must be remembered that the fathers were skilled in reading some phases of the Indian mind. They knew that an accident to the Cross might work a complete revolution in the minds of the superstitious Indians whose conversion they sought. Hence common, practical sense demanded speedy and easy access to the cross in case such emergency arose.

It will also be noticed that throughout the whole chain of Missions the walls, piers and buttresses are exceedingly solid and massive, reaching even to six, eight, ten and more feet in thickness. This was undoubtedly for the purpose of counteracting the shaking of the earthquakes, and the effectiveness of this method of building is evidenced by the fact that these old adobe structures still remain (even though some are in a shattered condition, owing to their long want of care) while later and more pretentious buildings have fallen.

From these details, therefore, it is apparent that the chief features of the Mission style of architecture are found to be as follows:

1. Solid and massive walls, piers and buttresses.
2. Arched corridors.
3. Curved pedimented gables.
4. Terraced towers, surmounted by a lantern.
5. Pierced Campanile, either in tower or wall.
6. Broad, unbroken, mural masses.
7. Wide, overhanging eaves.
8. Long, low, sloping roofs covered with red clay tiles.
9. Patio, or inner court.

In studying carefully the whole chain of Missions in California I found that the only building that contains all these elements in harmonious combination is that of San Luis Rey. Hence it alone is to be regarded as the typical Mission structure, all the others failing in one or more essentials. Santa Barbara is spoiled as a pure piece of Mission architecture by the introduction of the Greek engaged columns in the *fachada*. San Juan Capistrano undoubtedly was a pure " type " structure, but in its present dilapidated condition it is almost impossible to determine its exact appearance.

San Antonio de Padua lacks the terraced towers and the pierced campanile. San Gabriel and Santa Inés also have no towers, though both have the pierced campanile. And so, on analysis, will all the Missions be found to be defective in one or more points and therefore not entitled to rank as " type " structures.

As an offshoot from the Mission style has come the now world-famed and popular California bungalow style, which appropriates to itself every architectural style and no-style known.

But California has also utilized to a remarkable degree in greater or lesser purity the distinctive features of the Mission style, as I have above enumerated them, in modern churches, hospitals, school-houses, railway depots, warehouses, private residences, court-houses, libraries, etc.

Of greater importance, however, than the de-

HIGH SCHOOL, RIVERSIDE, CALIF.

In modern Mission architecture.

Photograph by C.C. Pierce & Co., Los Angeles.

WALL DECORATIONS ON OLD MISSION CHAPEL OF SAN ANTONIO DE PALA.

ARCHES AT GLENWOOD MISSION INN, RIVERSIDE, CALIF.

velopment of what I regard as a distinct style of architecture, is the development of the Mission *spirit* in architecture. Copying of past styles is never a proof of originality or power. The same spirit that led to the creation of the Mission Style, — the creative impulse, the originality, the vision, the free, imaginative power, the virility that desires expression and demands objective manifestation, — *this* was fostered by the Franciscan architects. This spirit is in the California atmosphere. A considerable number of architects have caught it. Without slavish adherence to any style, without copying anything, they are creating, expressing, even as did the Franciscan padres, beautiful thoughts in stone, brick, wood and reinforced concrete. In my *magnum opus* on *Mission Architecture*, which has long been in preparation, I hope clearly to present not only the full details of what the padres accomplished, but what these later creative artists, impelled by the same spirit, have given to the world.

CHAPTER XXXIV

THE GLENWOOD MISSION INN

IT is an incontrovertible fact that no great idea ever rests in its own accomplishment. There are offshoots from it, ideas generated in other minds entirely different from the original, yet dependent upon it for life. For instance, which of the Mission fathers had the faintest conception that in erecting their structures under the adverse conditions then existing in California, they were practically originating a new style of architecture; or that in making their crude and simple chairs, benches and tables they were starting a revolution in furniture making; or that in caring for and entertaining the few travelers who happened to pass over *El Camino Real* they were to suggest a name, an architectural style, a method of management for the most unique, and in many respects the most attractive hotel in the world. For such indeed is the Glenwood Mission Inn, at Riverside, California, at this present time.

This inn is an honest and just tribute to the influence of the Old Mission Fathers of California, as necessary to a complete understanding of the far-reaching power of their work as is *El*

Camino Real, the Mission Play, or the Mission Style of architecture. After listening to lectures on the work of the Franciscan padres and visiting the Missions themselves, its owners, Mr. and Mrs. Frank Miller, humanely interested in the welfare of the Mission Indians, collectors of the handicrafts of these artistic aborigines, and students of what history tells us of them, began, some twenty-five years ago, to realize that in the Mission idea was an ideal for a modern hotel. Slowly the suggestion grew, and as they discussed it with those whose knowledge enabled them to appreciate it, the clearer was it formulated, until some ten or a dozen years ago time seemed ripe for its realization. Arthur B. Benton, one of the leading architects of Southern California, formulated plans, and the hotel was erected. Its architecture conforms remarkably to that of the Missions. On Seventh Street are the arched corridors of San Fernando, San Juan Capistrano, San Miguel and San Antonio de Padua; inside is an extensive patio and the automobiles stop close to the Campanile reproducing the curved pediments of San Gabriel. On the Sixth Street side is the *fachada* of Santa Barbara Mission, and over the corner of Sixth and Orange Streets is the imposing dome of San Carlos Borromeo in the Carmelo Valley, flanked by buttresses of solid concrete, copies of those of San Gabriel.

The walls throughout are massive and unbroken by any other lines than those of doors, windows

and eaves, and the roofs are covered with red tiles.
In the Bell Tower a fine chime of bells is placed,
the playing of which at noon and sunset recalls
the matins and vespers of the Mission days.

Within the building, the old Mission atmosphere
is wonderfully preserved.   In the Cloister Music
Room the windows are of rare and exquisite stained
glass, showing St. Cecilia, the seats are cathedral
stalls of carved oak; the rafters are replicas of the
wooden beams of San Miguel, and the balcony
is copied from the chancel rail of the same Mission.   Mission sconces, candelabra, paintings,
banners, etc., add to the effect, while the floor is
made in squares of oak with mahogany par-
quetry to remind the visitor of the square tile
pavements found in several of the old Missions.

Daily — three times — music is called forth
from the cathedral organ and harp, and one may
hear music of every type, from the solemn, stately
harmonies of the German choral, the crashing
thunders of Bach's fugues and Passion music, to
the light oratorios, and duets and solos of Pergo-
lesi.

By the side of the Music Room is the Cloistered
Walk, divided into sections, in each of which some
distinctive epoch or feature of Mission history
is represented by mural paintings by modern
artists of skill and power.   The floor is paved with
tiles from one of the abandoned Missions.

Beyond is the Refectorio, or dining-room of an
ancient Mission, containing a collection of kitchen

and dining utensils, some of them from Moorish times. It has a stone ceiling, groined arches, and harvest festival windows, which also represent varied characters, scenes, industries and recreations connected with old Mission life.

Three other special features of the Mission Inn are its wonderful collection of crosses, of bells, and the Ford paintings. Any one of these would grace the halls of a national collection of rare and valuable antiques. Of the crosses it can truthfully be said that they form the largest and most varied collection in the world, and the bells have been the subject of several articles in leading magazines.

The Ford paintings are a complete representation of all the Missions and were made by Henry Chapman Ford, of Santa Barbara, mainly during the years 1880–1881, though some of them are dated as early as 1875.

The Glenwood Mission Inn proved so popular that in the summer and fall of 1913 two new wings were added, surrounding a Spanish Court. This Court has cloisters on two sides and cloistered galleries above, and is covered with Spanish tile, as it is used for an open air dining-room. One of the new wings, a room 100 feet long by 30 feet wide, and three stories high, with coffered ceiling, is a Spanish Art Gallery. Here are displayed old Spanish pictures and tapestries, many of which were collected by Mr. Miller personally on his European and Mexican trips.

At the same time the dining-room was enlarged by more than half its former capacity, one side of it looking out through large French windows on the cloisters and the court itself. This necessitated the enlargement of the kitchen which is now thrown open to the observation of the guests whenever desired.

Taking it all in all, the Glenwood Mission Inn is not only a unique and delightful hostelry, but a wonderful manifestation of the power of the Franciscan friars to impress their spirit and life upon the commercial age of a later and more material civilization.

CHAPTER XXXV

THE INTERIOR DECORATIONS OF THE MISSIONS

WE cannot to-day determine how the Franciscans of the Southwest decorated the interiors of all
their churches. Some of these buildings have
disappeared entirely, while others have been
restored or renovated beyond all semblance of their
original condition. But enough are left to give
us a satisfactory idea of the labors of the fathers
and of their subject Indians. At the outset,
it must be confessed that while the fathers understood well the principles of architecture and created a natural, spontaneous style, meeting all obstacles of time and place which presented themselves, they showed little skill in matters of interior decoration, possessing neither originality
in design, the taste which would have enabled them
to become good copyists, nor yet the slightest
appreciation of color-harmony. In making this
criticism, I do not overlook the difficulties in the
way of the missionaries, or the insufficiency of
materials at command. The priests were as much
hampered in this work as they were in that of
building. But, in the one case, they met with

brilliant success; in the other they failed. The decorations have, therefore, a distinctly pathetic quality. They show a most earnest endeavor to beautify what to those who wrought them was the very house of God. Here mystically dwelt the very body, blood, and reality of the Object of Worship. Hence the desire to glorify the dwelling-place of their God, and their own temple. The great distance in this case between desire and performance is what makes the result pathetic. Instead of trusting to themselves, or reverting to first principles, as they did in architecture, the missionaries endeavored to reproduce from memory the ornaments with which they had been familiar in their early days in Spain. They remembered decorations in Catalonia, Cantabria, Mallorca, Burgos, Valencia, and sought to imitate them; having neither exactitude nor artistic qualities to fit them for their task. No amount of kindliness can soften this decision. The results are to be regretted; for I am satisfied that, had the fathers trusted to themselves, or sought for simple nature-inspirations, they would have given us decorations as admirable as their architecture. What I am anxious to emphasize in this criticism is the principle involved. Instead of originating or relying upon nature, they copied without intelligence. The rude brick, adobe, or rubble work, left in the rough, or plastered and whitewashed, would have been preferable to their unmeaning patches of color. In the one, there would have been rugged

THE OLD ALTAR AT THE CHAPEL OF SAN ANTONIO DE PALA.

Showing original wall decorations prized by the Indians.

ALTAR AND INTERIOR OF CHAPEL OF SAN ANTONIO DE PALA, AFTER REMOVAL OF WALL
DECORATIONS PRIZED BY INDIANS.

strength to admire; in the other there exists only pretense to condemn.

After this criticism was written I asked for the opinion of the learned and courteous Father Zephyrin, the Franciscan historian. In reply the following letter was received, which so clearly gives another side to the matter that I am glad to quote it entire:

" I do not think your criticism from an artistic view is too severe; but it would have been more just to judge the decorations as you would the efforts of amateurs, and then to have made sure as to their authors.

" You assume that they were produced by the padres themselves. This is hardly demonstrable. They probably gave directions, and some of them, in their efforts to make things plain to the crude mind of the Indians, may have tried their hands at work to which they were not trained any more than clerical candidates or university students are at the present time; but it is too much to assume that those decorations give evidence even of the taste of the fathers. In that matter, as in everything else that was not contrary to faith or morals, they adapted themselves to the taste of their wards, or very likely, too, to the humor of such stray ' artists ' as might happen upon the coast, or whom they might be able to import. You must bear in mind that in all California down to 1854 there were no lay-brothers accompanying the fathers to perform such work as is done by our lay-brothers now, who can very well compete with the best of secular artisans. The church of St. Boniface, San Francisco, and the church

of St. Joseph, Los Angeles, are proof of this. Hence the
fathers were left to their own wits in giving general
directions, and to the taste of white 'artists,' and
allowed even Indians to suit themselves. You will
find this all through ancient Texas, New Mexico, and
Arizona. The Indians loved the gaudy, loud, grotesque,
and as it was the main thing for the fathers to gain the
Indians in any lawful way possible, the taste of the
latter was paramount.

" As your criticism stands, it cannot but throw a slur
upon the poor missionaries, who after all did not put
up these buildings and have them decorated as they did
for the benefit of future critics, but for the instruction
and pleasure of the natives. Having been an Indian missionary myself, I acted just so. I have found that
the natives would not appreciate a work of art, whereas
they prized the grotesque. Well, as long as it drew
them to prize the supernatural more, what difference
did it make to the missionary? You yourself refer to
the unwise action of the Pala priest in not considering
the taste and the affection of the Indians."

Another critic of my criticism insists that,
" while the Indians, if left to themselves, possess
harmony of color which seems never to fail, they
always demand startling effects from us." This,
I am inclined to question. The Indians' color-
sense in their basketry is perfect, as also in their
blankets, and I see no reason for the assumption
that they should demand of us what is manifestly
so contrary to their own natural and normal tastes.

It must, in justice to the padres, be confessed
that, holding the common notions on decoration,

ALTAR AND CEILING DECORATIONS, MISSION SANTA INES.

Photograph by Howard Tibbitts, San Francisco.
INTERIOR OF MISSION SAN FRANCISCO DE ASIS, SHOWING MURAL AND
CEILING DECORATIONS.

it is often harder to decorate a house than it is to build it; but why decorate at all? The dull color of the natural adobe, or plaster, would have at least been true art in its simple dignity of architecture, whereas when covered with unmeaning designs in foolish colors even the architectural dignity is detracted from.

One writer says that the colors used in these interior decorations were mostly of vegetable origin and were sized with glue. The yellows were extracted from poppies, blues from nightshade, though the reds were gained from stones picked up from the beach. The glue was manufactured on the spot from the bones, etc., of the animals slaughtered for food.

As examples of interior decoration, the Missions of San Miguel Arcángel and Santa Inés are the only ones that afford opportunity for extended study. At Santa Clara, the decorations of the ceiling were restored as nearly like the original as possible, but with modern colors and workmanship. At Pala Chapel the priest whitewashed the mural distemper paintings out of existence. A small patch remains at San Juan Bautista merely as an example; while a splashed and almost obliterated fragment is the only survival at San Carlos Carmelo.

At San Miguel, little has been done to disturb the interior, so that it is in practically the same condition as it was left by the padres themselves. Fr. Zephyrin informs me that these decorations were done by one Murros, a Spaniard, whose daughter, Mrs. McKee, at the age of over eighty, is still alive at Monterey. She told him that the work was done in 1820 or 1821. He copied the designs out of books, she says, and none but Indians assisted him in the actual work, though the padres were fully consulted as it progressed.

At Santa Barbara all that remains of the old decorations are found in the reredos, the marble-izing of the engaged columns on each wall and the entrance and side arches. This marble effect is exceedingly rude, and does not represent the color of any known marble.

In the old building of San Francisco the rafters of the ceiling have been allowed to retain their ancient decorations. These consist of rhomboidal figures placed conventionally from end to end of the building.

At Santa Clara, when the church was restored in 1861–1862, and again in 1885, the original decorations on walls and ceiling were necessarily destroyed or injured. But where possible they were kept intact; where injured, retouched; and where destroyed, replaced as near the original as the artist could accomplish. In some cases the original work was on canvas, and some on wood. Where this could be removed and replaced it was done. The retouching was done by an Italian artist who came down from San Francisco.

On the walls, the wainscot line is set off with the sinuous body of the serpent, which not only lends

INTERIOR OF MISSION SAN MIGUEL FROM THE CHOIR GALLERY

Photograph by C.C. Pierce & Co., Los Angeles.

FACHADA OF MISSION CHAPEL AT LOS ANGELES.

ARCHES SOUTHERN PACIFIC RAILWAY DEPOT,
SANTA BARBARA, CALIF.

itself well to such a purpose of ornamentation, but was a symbolic reminder to the Indians of that old serpent, the devil, the father of lies and evil, who beguiled our first parents in the Garden of Eden.

In the ruins of the San Fernando church faint traces of the decorations of the altar can still be seen in two simple rounded columns, with cornices above.

At San Juan Capistrano, on the east side of the quadrangle, in the northeast corner, is a small room; and in one corner of this is a niche for a statue, the original decorations therein still remaining. It is weather-stained, and the rain has washed the adobe in streaks over some of it; yet it is interesting. It consists of a rude checker-board design, or, rather, of a diagonal lozenge pattern in reds and yellows.

There are also a few remnants of the mural distemper paintings in the altar zone of the ruined church.

CHAPTER XXXVI

HOW TO REACH THE MISSIONS

SAN DIEGO. From Los Angeles to San Diego, Santa Fé Railway, 126 miles, one way fare $3.85; round trip $5.00, good ten days; or $7.00, good 30 days, with stop-over privileges at Oceanside, which allows a visit to San Luis Rey and Pala (via Oceanside) and San Juan Capistrano. Or steamship, $3.00 and $2.25; round trip, first class, $5.25. The Mission is six miles from San Diego, and a carriage must be taken all the way, or the electric car to the bluff, fare five cents; thence by Bluff Road, on burro, two miles, fare fifty cents. The better way is to drive by Old Town and return by the Bluff Road.

SAN LUIS REY. From Los Angeles to Oceanside, Santa Fé Railway, 85 miles, fare $2.55; round trip, ten days, $4.60. Take carriage from livery, or walk to Mission, 4 miles. The trip to Pala may be taken at the same time, though sleeping accommodations are uncertain at Pala. Meals may be had at one or two of the Indian houses, as a rule.

SAN JUAN CAPISTRANO. From Los Angeles to Capistrano, Santa Fé Railway, 58 miles, fare

$1.70. The Mission is close to the station. Hotel accommodations are poor.

SAN GABRIEL. From Los Angeles to San Gabriel, Southern Pacific Railway, 8 miles, fare 25 cents. Or Pacific electric car from Los Angeles, 25 cents.

SAN FERNANDO. From Los Angeles to San Fernando, Southern Pacific Railway, 21 miles, fare 65 cents. Thence by carriage or on foot or horseback to the Mission, 1½ miles. Livery and hotel at San Fernando.

SAN BUENAVENTURA. From Los Angeles to San Buenaventura, Southern Pacific Railway, 76 miles, fare $2.30. Or steamship, $2.35, special, Saturday to Monday, $3.00 round trip. Electric cars from Southern Pacific Station pass the Mission.

SANTA BARBARA. From Los Angeles to Santa Barbara, Southern Pacific Railway, fare $3.15; special round trip, Saturday to Monday, $3.50. From San Francisco to Santa Barbara, 370 miles, Southern Pacific Railway, fare $13.40 and $11.65. Street car passes the Mission.

SANTA INÉS. This is not on the line of any railway. It can be reached from Santa Barbara, 25 miles, by carriage, or from Los Olivos, four miles, by stage. Los Olivos is on the line of the Pacific Coast Railway. To reach it take Southern Pacific Railway to San Luis Obispo, change cars. It is then 66 miles to Los Olivos, fare $3.00. The better way is to go by Southern Pacific to Lompoc, take carriage and visit the site of Old La Purísima, then Purísima, then drive to Santa Inés and return. With a good team this can be done in a day. Distance 25 miles.

LA PURÍSIMA CONCEPCIÓN. Go to Lompoc on the coast line of the Southern Pacific either from Los Angeles (181 miles, $5.60) or San Francisco (294 miles, $9.35). Carriage from livery to the ruins of Old Purísima, thence to the later one, five miles.

SAN LUIS OBISPO. Southern Pacific Railway from either Los Angeles (222 miles, $6.70) or San Francisco (253 miles, $7.30), or steamship to Port Hartford and the Pacific Coast Railway, 211 miles, $6.50. The Mission is in the town.

SAN MIGUEL. The Mission is but a few rods from the Southern Pacific Station, reached either from Los Angeles (273 miles, $8.05) or San Francisco (208 miles, $5.95). By far the better way, however, is to go to Paso Robles, where one can bathe in the Hot Springs so noted even in Indian days, while enjoying the hospitalities of one of the best hotels on the Pacific Coast. Carriages may be secured from one of the livery stables. From here visit Santa Isabel Ranch and Hot Springs (which used to belong to San Miguel), then drive 16 miles to San Miguel. On account of the completeness of its interior decorations, this is, in many respects, especially to the student, the most interesting Mission of the whole chain.

SAN ANTONIO DE PADUA. It is a twenty-mile

THE CITY HALL, SANTA MONICA, CALIF.

MISSION CHAPEL AT LOS ANGELES, FROM THE PLAZA PARK.

RESIDENCE IN LOS ANGELES, CALIF.

Showing influence of Mission style of architecture.

stage ride from King's City, on the line of the Southern Pacific (216 miles from Los Angeles, $9.35) to Jolon (fare $2.00), the quaintest little village now remaining in California, which is practically the gateway to Mission San Antonio de Padua. At Jolon one secures a team, and, after a six-mile drive through a beautiful park, dotted on every hand with majestic live-oaks, — ancient monarchs that have accumulated moss and majesty with their years, — the ruins of the old Mission come into view. From San Francisco to King's City is 164 miles, fare $4.65.

LA SOLEDAD. The Mission is four miles from the town of Soledad on the Southern Pacific Railway. From Los Angeles, 337 miles, fare $9.95. From San Francisco, 144 miles, fare $4.00. Livery from Soledad to the Mission.

SAN JUAN BAUTISTA is six miles from Sargent's Station on the Southern Pacific. Two stages run daily, fare $1.00 for the round trip. Visitors may be accommodated at the Plaza Hotel, conducted by William Haydon. From Los Angeles to Sargent's, 394 miles, fare $11.65. From San Francisco, 87 miles, fare $2.35.

SAN CARLOS BORROMEO, MONTEREY. The old presidio church is in the town of Monterey, and reached by car-line from Hotel del Monte or the town. San Carlos Carmelo is about six miles from Monterey, and must be reached by carriage or automobile. By far the best way is to stop at either Hotel del Monte or Hotel Carmelo, Pacific Grove, and then on taking the seventeen-mile drive, make the side trip to San Carlos. To Monterey from San Francisco, on the Southern Pacific Railway, is 126 miles, fare $3.00. Friday to Tuesday excursion, round trip, $4.50. From Los Angeles to Monterey, Southern Pacific Railway, 398 miles, fare $11.45.

Santa Cruz. It is well to go from San Francisco on the narrow gauge, 80 miles, Southern Pacific, and return on the broad gauge, 121 miles. Fare on either line $2.80. On the narrow gauge are the Big Trees, at which an interesting stopover can be enjoyed.

Santa Clara. While there is a city of Santa Clara it is better to go to San José (the first town established in California), and stay at Hotel Vendome, and then drive or go by electric car, down the old Alameda to Santa Clara Mission, 3½ miles.

Mission San José. So called to distinguish it from the city of San José. By Southern Pacific Railway from San Francisco to Irvington, 34 miles, fare 85 cents. Or from the city of San José, 14 miles by Southern Pacific, or a pleasant carriage drive. From Irvington to the Mission, three miles, stage twice daily, fare 25 cents.

San Francisco de Asis is on Sixteenth and Dolores Streets, three miles from Palace Hotel. Take Valencia or Howard electric cars.

San Rafael. There is nothing left at San Rafael of the old Mission. The town is reached by North Pacific Coast Railway, 18 miles, or California Northwestern, 15 miles, fare 35 cents.

SAN FRANCISCO SOLANO is in the town of Sonoma. Reached by North Pacific Coast Railway, 43 miles, fare $1.00

THE END.